"A porn plague is raging in homes a[...] across the world today, and b[...]ery addicted husband there is a brokenh[...]ed wife. While [...] is an abundance of powerful, biblical resources to help men overcome addiction, their wives have largely been overlooked. I am grateful that Vicki Tiede has filled that void. In a book that is sensitive, biblical, and conversational, she comes alongside hurting women as a friend and guides them to the hope and peace only the gospel can give."

Tim Challies, Pastor; blogger; author of *Sexual Detox: A Guide for Guys Who Are Sick of Porn*

"This is an outstanding, significant, invaluable, and essential resource for today's women and particularly today's Christian women. (I am confident that men would benefit from reading it also.) Vicki presents hard information in a most gracious and gentle way. She is relational and honestly cares about the women who will be reading this book. She conveys an earnest desire to be a comforting resource to those suffering with a wounded heart. I recommend this book as a source of comfort, strength, and hope. It is saturated with Scripture and prayer."

Elsie E. Woolf, M.A., Board Certified Christian Counselor, National Coalition For Purity

"When your world is rocked by your husband's infidelity, God can seem far away and Scripture dry. This book will be a breath of fresh air during those days. Having been in that situation, Vicki earns the right to challenge us to turn to the true Source of our hope, strength, and healing. Her blend of hopeful stories, helpful information, and pure Bible study fills a gap in the healing journey not seen in other materials."

Melissa Williams, Women's Director, Pure Life Alliance

"*Heartfelt, restoration,* and *complete* are the words I would use to describe this book. It is by far the most thorough book on helping a woman deal with her husband's struggle with pornography. As I read the book, I could see the restoration happening in women's lives. Each chapter (week) leads you to the next step in getting your life and relationship with God back on track. Vicki's comment at the beginning of the book is 'The purpose of this book is to take you on a journey to discover how your broken heart can become a work of splendor in the masterful hands of God.' As a man who has broken trust with his own wife, this book made me realize that it was important for me to see the full betrayal this addiction has on a marriage. My recommendation is that every man who is serious about restoring his relationship with his wife reads this book after his wife has finished it. He will see his pornography addiction in a completely different way—and that will be a good thing."

Brent Barrowcliff, Transparent Ministries,
www.transparentministries.org;
Freedom Begins Here, www.freedombeginshere.org

"Vicki Tiede has come alongside the millions of wives whose husbands are addicted to porn, to bind up their broken hearts and give them hope—as only one who has been there can."

Bob Tiede, Director of Global Operations Leadership Development
for Campus Crusade for Christ International

"If you are one of the increasing numbers of women who have discovered their husband losing the battle with pornography, Vicki Tiede gives you an informed, practical guide offering Christ-centered hope and restoration. Be sure to make this book a part of your journey to healing."

Michael John Cusick, author of *Surfing for God:*
Discovering Divine Desire Beneath Sexual Struggle

"Vicki Tiede guides, comforts, and encourages hurting and heart-bruised wives to 'fix your eyes on the One who calms the storms and stills the raging seas, and find peace in the midst of it all.' I've been refreshed and helped in my own ministry to hurting women by this book which clearly and compassionately points us to the grace of Jesus Christ and the healing power of his Word."

Ellen Dykas, Women's Ministry Coordinator for Harvest USA
www.harvestusa.org; editor of *Sexual Sanity for Women*

"I will recommend this book for women to read. It will serve as a valued addition to therapy, and the thoughtful questions interspersed throughout the book are rich opportunities for exploring feelings, truth, and faith further. The author has an easy-to-read writing style and has tackled a difficult subject with grace and truth."

Margaret P Moore, MA, LMFT, LADC, RN, Licensed Marriage
and Family Therapist, Experiencing Moore, LLC

WHEN YOUR HUSBAND IS ADDICTED TO PORNOGRAPHY

HEALING YOUR WOUNDED HEART

Vicki Tiede

New
Growth
Press

New Growth Press, Greensboro, NC 27404
www.newgrowthpress.com
Copyright © 2012 by Vicki Tiede

Unless otherwise indicated, Scripture quotations are taken from *The Holy Bible,
English Standard Version.*® Copyright © 2000; 2001 by Crossway Bibles, a
division of Good News Publishers. Used by permission. All rights reserved.

Scripture quotations marked NIV are taken from the *Holy Bible, New
International Version*®. *NIV*®. Copyright © 1973, 1978, 1984 by International
Bible Society. Used by permission of Zondervan. All rights reserved.

Scripture quotations marked KJV are taken from the King James Version of
the Bible.

Scripture quotations marked NASB are taken from the *New American Standard
Bible,* © Copyright 1960, 1962, 1963, 1968, 1971, 1972, 1973, 1975, 1977,
1995 by The Lockman Foundation. Used by permission.

Cover Design: Brandon Hill Design, bhilldesign.com
Interior Design and Typesetting: North Market Street Graphics

ISBN 978-1-936768-63-9
ISBN 978-1-936768-58-5 (ebook)

Library of Congress Cataloging-in-Publication Data

Tiede, Vicki, 1967–
When your husband is addicted to pornograpy : healing your wounded heart /
Vicki Tiede.
      p.   cm.
Includes bibliographical references and index.
ISBN 978-1-936768-63-9 (alk. paper)
1. Pornography—Religious aspects—Christianity—
Textbooks.   2. Husbands—Sexual behavior.—Textbooks.   3. Christian
men—Sexual behavior.—Textbooks.   I. Title.
BV4597.6.T54 2012
241'.667—dc23

                                        2012018321

Printed in the United States of America

23 22 21 20 19 18 17 16   6 7 8 9 10

This book is dedicated to
every woman who is seeking hope and healing
in the midst of her husband's addiction
and
to Jesus,
for putting my heart back together and
making something beautiful out of my mess.
I'll love you, trust you, and follow you forever.

Acknowledgments

A book this honest and sensitive could have been written only with the support of many treasured people.

Blythe Daniel, my outstanding literary agent, thank you for believing in me and in this project. Your encouragement, friendship, and expertise arc priceless.

To my new friends at New Growth Press, I am so excited to be collaborating with you. I can't wait to see what God is going to do. Sue Lutz, thank you for gently smoothing out the rough spots and polishing my words to a shine.

I could not have written this book without the family members and friends who made up my team of faithful prayer warriors. On the dark days when I was reliving deep sadness from my own story in order to remember my healing journey, you were on your knees seeking the face of the Healer of broken hearts. On the days when I pushed my chair away from the computer and wept tears of joy because the writing that day had been particularly sweet, you were standing in the gap, giving praise to the Giver of Joy.

To my church family at Calvary Evangelical Free Church, on a regular basis you helped meet our family's daily needs with carpooling, meals, playdates, and red licorice (my writing companion). Thank you. You demonstrated to our family what a close, loving, caring community is supposed to look like.

This book is filled with stories from incredibly brave women who dared to share their deepest hurts. Because your stories are personal and I desire to protect your privacy, I am not able to list your names, but you know who you are. I am forever grateful for your transparency and willingness to be vulnerable so that other women will know without a doubt that they are not alone. A special thanks to those who took the extra measure of reading the manuscript as it was being written and baring your heart even further by sharing your responses with me. Your transparency shaped this book.

My pastor and friend, Kevin Barnhart, I thank you for reading my manuscript and sharing your insightful comments. Your encouragement and support during the writing process was practical and indefatigable.

My sister-in-Christ and first reader, Tracy Ruckman, words can't begin to express my deep appreciation for your contribution to this book. Our almost daily communication sustained me as I wrote. You encouraged my heart, read my manuscript as fast as I could type it, and helped me turn the words of my heart into something God could use. I love you, dear friend.

Mom and Dad, anything good God chooses to do in my life has its roots in you. You were my first teachers, showing me by example what marriage is supposed to look like. You bore the pain of parenting an adult child with a shattered heart, and you celebrated the journey of its restoration. Thank you. I love you more than I can say.

Kadi, Ben, and Caleb, you are each a gift of grace in my life. You have shaped me as we've laughed, cried, and learned together. Thank you for picking up extra chores and providing me with constant welcomed distractions while I wrote this book. I will love you forever.

Finally, my most heartfelt thanks go to my husband, Mike. You gave me permission to write honestly about my experience before you were in my life, with full knowledge that the title of this book would cause people to look at you differently. You have handled every step with grace. When I sobbed in your arms because I was so angry that God would ask me to write about this painful subject, you soothed my hurting heart with your words and your prayers. You have been my constant encourager, my partner, and my friend. I can't imagine life without you. You are truly the one my soul loves.

Most of all, I thank Jesus, my Healer. This is my offering to you. *Soli Deo Gloria.*

Contents

Contents

Week 4 • Identity

Week 5 • Brokenness

Week 6 • Forgiveness

Introduction

As I sit here with my fingers poised over the keys, ready to write what God is calling me to write, I am reminded of Christ's final hours before he was crucified. As the crowds followed him, surely they thought Golgotha was the last mountain Christ would climb. They were wrong. When he climbed his last mountain, he never stopped until he was in glory with the Father.

If you are reading this introduction, it's most likely because God has unveiled your husband's secret addiction to lust, masturbation, and pornography. Perhaps I am the first to say this to you: I'm so sorry. I'm sorry for all the feelings you have experienced that have risen from the depths of your toes and threatened to strangle you. My heart breaks for the things you've seen, the choices you've had to make, and the ramifications of this addiction on your marriage and your family.

This mountain in your life may look like Golgotha, but if you have Jesus as your Lord and Savior, this mountain only makes possible your Mount of Olives—the place where you stand in the presence of your Father.

This book is not meant to give you tools and skills to fix your husband. It is for and about *you*, not your husband.

When Your Husband Is Addicted to Pornography addresses six themes: hope, surrender, trust, identity, brokenness, and forgiveness. Rather than dividing the book into chapters, I divided it into weeks. Each week addresses one theme. The six weeks are further broken into five days of reading and contemplation. You may approach the text in a variety of ways. You might read it exactly as it's written, completing one week's theme in one calendar week, or you might choose to linger on a particular day or week of reading for a longer period before moving on. You might also read the book straight through at a quicker pace and then cycle back through it a second time to work through the questions. Perhaps you have a friend on a similar journey and you will choose to go through the book together. In other words, I hope you will approach this book in whatever way works best for you. Just please take the time to make it truly meaningful by answering the application questions.

To be sure we are speaking the same language as you read, I want to define the four levels of sexual addiction I will describe in this book. Dr. Patrick Carnes, a nationally known speaker and author on sexual addictions, identified three levels of addiction in his book *Out of the Shadows: Understanding Sexual Addiction.* I've chosen to divide his Level I category into two levels.

Level I: This is often considered "acceptable" by mainstream society and includes lust, fantasy, masturbation, and pornography (magazines, video, cable/satellite TV, Internet).

Level II: Fulfilling sexual desire with live porn: strip clubs, nude dancing, massage parlors, physical affairs, and fetishes.

Level III: Criminal behavior including voyeurism, exhibitionism, phone sex, inappropriate touching, and prostitution.

Level IV: Violent criminal behavior including sexual assault, rape, and child molestation.

As I did my research for this book, I interacted with twenty-five women who were willing to be part of a focus group. They completed an extensive questionnaire, participated in an interview, and read and completed the questions on each chapter as I wrote them. At least 25 percent of the husbands represented in this group exhibited behaviors from Levels II–IV. One hundred percent of those men started at Level I.

This book is for women whose husbands have engaged in Level I sexual behaviors. If you are aware that your husband has struggled with lust, fantasy, pornography, and/or masturbation now or in the past, this book is for you.

If your husband has engaged in Level II–IV behaviors, this book is also for you. I want to be clear, however, that the primary focus of the book will be to deal with our own issues and feelings regarding a husband's lust, masturbation, and pornography. It will only minimally address issues in Levels II–IV. Therefore, if your husband has had an affair, paid for prostitutes, or raped someone, and you are looking for a book that will focus on those specific issues, it will not be this book. However, many of the feelings you have, the ramifications of these behaviors on your relationship with your husband, and the needs you are experiencing are addressed in this book, and I pray that you will be blessed by what God teaches you here.

This book is not a handbook for fixing your husband. However, I'm very aware that you may be seeking information specific to your situation. In the appendix I have listed numerous nonfiction books that I encourage you to investigate. I have also listed sexual addiction ministries, online resources, and counseling opportunities for you to prayerfully consider.

In the end you are only responsible for yourself and the choices you make. Sometimes in life you have to make the best decision you know how to make, given the information you have at the time. When my first husband did not take responsibility for his actions or recognize a need to repent of his behavior, the behavior escalated, and my emotional, physical, and spiritual health was at risk. I was advised by a Christian counselor and my pastor to end the marriage, and I did. Please hear me when I say this: God hates divorce (Malachi 2:16 NIV), and I have never met anyone who has gone through a divorce who doesn't agree with God on this one. It is God's desire that every heart and marriage be restored (Job 22:23). Some issues may make a marriage irreconcilable, but the purpose of this book is not to point you in that direction. Rather, it is to point you to the One who can bring about restoration and reconciliation.

I decided to write this book for women who want and need to know that there is hope and that God is big enough to meet all of their needs. However, this subject is extremely sensitive and complicated, and many women and couples will need outside assistance. The appendix contains information on how you can find the right assistance.

I thank God that you are holding this book in your hands right now. You are not alone. As you make your way through this book, you will meet many other women who have experienced the same hurt and betrayal you are experiencing. I pray that you will find the help and hope you need in these pages.

My prayer is that you will focus your eyes on the God of hope rather than base your hope and happiness on your husband's choices. Learning to allow God to meet your greatest needs is a long process, probably longer than this six-week book. It's a slow dance through brokenness in the arms of the Almighty. I know. I have been in your shoes, and I have learned the intricate steps to finding hope in the midst of a husband's addiction to pornography.

Our God longs to meet you in the center of your pain. He can handle your tears. He knows your anger. He understands the feelings you are experiencing. He was "a man of sorrows and acquainted with grief" (Isaiah 53:3 KJV).

I invite you to step into the embrace of Jesus as you face your Golgotha. The sin has been unveiled. Now allow Jesus to reveal God's grace, truth, and hope as he leads you into the Father's presence, picking up the pieces of your broken heart and creating a new mosaic heart that reflects the beauty and grace of the Redeemer.

I have used the *English Standard Version* of the Bible unless otherwise noted. If you do not own the *ESV,* you will still be able to answer nearly every question without confusion.

HOPE

WEEK 1

Day 1: Truth Unveiled

Greg has always been a little unfocused. I've noticed that he's often inordinately distracted at the checkout counter, and he lingers on racy scenes longer than necessary when surfing TV channels. I've chalked it up as normal guy behavior our whole marriage.

When I caught him lying to me about petty things, I concluded that I was married to Peter Pan. Why else would he tell a ridiculous story about working late and not being hungry after missing dinner, when, according to the receipt left in his jeans pocket, he was at a gas station buying a donut and Dew at dinnertime? There was no point in confronting him; it wasn't worth it. He was just a boy who didn't want to grow up.

Then one afternoon as I puttered around on the computer, I discovered a new tool our Internet provider offered. In the Favorites menu, it automatically created and displayed all of the sites most frequently visited so the user could easily return to them. The more frequently a site was visited, the higher it appeared on the list. To my shock and horror, there was a lengthy list of pornography websites topping the list.

—Audrey

1

No doubt the beaming faces of your friends and family members reflected the joy on your own face as you walked down the aisle on your wedding day. Your heart overflowed with love for the handsome man waiting to exchange vows with you at the front of the church. You never felt more beautiful, loved, and desirable. Your mind was a warehouse of dreams and expectations for the rest of your days as Mrs. Right.

Then the unthinkable happened. Whether you have been married a few months or celebrated numerous milestone anniversaries, your "happily ever after" has been tarnished by the discovery of your husband's sexual addiction. Perhaps you stumbled upon something on the computer, or you unwittingly uncovered a secret stash of pornographic magazines and movies. Maybe you walked in on your husband in the middle of an act of self-gratification.

Each of our experiences is different. Our reactions, needs, and solutions will be different as well. How I wish I could peer into your life and offer you an individualized solution to your unique situation! I'd love to be able to say, "Friend, if you do X, then Y will happen." If you think that is what this book will provide, you are going to be sorely disappointed. I can't possibly offer that kind of hope and healing myself. However, I have walked in your shoes, and I know how desperately you long for a solution and some guarantees. I don't have the answers, but I know Who does.

I believe that the most pressing need we all share is to embrace the hope that God is able and willing to pluck us out of the slimy pit, remove the filth that's clinging to our hearts and minds, and usher us to the next step of healing. Amen?

For a while you didn't even know you were in a pit. Like undetected termites that eat away at a foundation until one day the house collapses, an ongoing sexual struggle has been undermining your home. God had to expose what was going on with your husband for you to rebuild on a firm foundation. As 1 Corinthians 4:5 says, God "will bring to light the things now hidden in darkness and will disclose the purposes of the heart."

Day 1: Truth Unveiled

While the discovery of your husband's sexual addiction pulled the rug out from under you, it came as no surprise to the Almighty. He sees the sins committed in a darkened office or bedroom just as clearly as those done in broad daylight.

It's not uncommon for a revelation to come as a complete surprise, however. Consider the apostle John. As an elderly man he was banished to the island of Patmos by the Roman authorities for faithfully preaching the gospel. In his wildest dreams, he probably never thought he'd meet Jesus on Patmos. The title of the book chronicling this experience is found in the first five words of Revelation: "The revelation of Jesus Christ" (Revelation 1:1). The Greek word for "Revelation" is *apokalupsis* (ä-po-kä'-lü-psēs), meaning "unveiled." God knows what has been unveiled in your current situation.

Read Daniel 2:22: "He reveals deep and hidden things; he knows what is in the darkness, and the light dwells with him."

What does God reveal?

What does he know?

How does it make you feel to realize that he knows and reveals things that were once hidden in secret?

Secrecy shrouds sexual addiction. Until a man confesses or is caught, his struggle with lust is his own burden to bear. For 70 percent of sex addicts, the Internet is the primary source of their pornography.[1] Online porn is extremely accessible, anonymous, and affordable, making it especially easy to hide. When your husband's addiction is made known to you, the secret becomes the albatross around *your* neck.

> I've been married for forty-five years and learned about my husband's struggle with masturbation two years after we were married. He's a good man, but he once said, "If this came to light, there would be nothing for a man to do but commit suicide." I felt so alone. For all these years, I couldn't tell a soul.
>
> —Esther

Read Psalm 44:21: "Would not God discover this? For he knows the secrets of the heart."

What does God know?

It sounds ridiculous to suggest that you should be grateful that God has unveiled the truth about your husband's addiction to you, but that's exactly what I'm going to do. Christ longs to set us free from the things that have been hiding in the shadows. To do so, those issues must be brought to light.

Read Ephesians 5:8–14 (NASB):

> For you were formerly darkness, but now you are Light in the Lord; walk as children of Light (for the fruit of the Light *consists* in all goodness and righteousness and truth), trying to learn what is pleasing to the Lord. Do not participate in the unfruitful deeds of darkness, but instead even expose them; for it is disgraceful even to speak of the things which are done by them in secret. But all things become visible when they are exposed by the light, for

everything that becomes visible is light. For this reason it says, "Awake, sleeper, and arise from the dead, and Christ will shine on you." (italics mine)

Verse eight is like the *Reader's Digest* version of the gospel, neatly wrapped up in one verse. Read the first half of the sentence very carefully: "For you were formerly darkness." Most of us tend to read what we *think* something should say or what we would prefer it to say rather than what it actually says. This passage reads, "You *were* . . . darkness," not "you were . . . *in* darkness." Ouch. But that makes sense in light of Paul's words to us in Romans 3:23, doesn't it? "For *all* have sinned and fall short of the glory of God" (emphasis added).

How are we to live according to the second part of verse 8?

What do you think that might look like for you right now in your circumstances?

What *doesn't* it look like?

(For the record, whenever I see the word "but" in Scripture, I find that it often means "That was the bad news, but here's the good news." It's certainly true in this passage.)

By what means are you now "Light"?

That little preposition "in" carries the meaning "through." We cross from being darkness to being light *through* Jesus Christ when God takes the wages of our sin and puts them on his Son instead of on us (Romans 6:23). Jesus took all our darkness onto himself and threw open the gates of heaven for us at the same time.

The second sentence in verse 8 tells us that in response to this amazing news we are to "Walk as children of Light, trying to learn what is pleasing to the Lord." Let's be honest: when we first learn of our husband's addiction or realize that he's relapsed into pornography after a period of sexual sobriety, we're not always sure how to "walk as children of Light." Living as children of Light doesn't feel natural when your emotions are off the charts. Feelings of rage, despair, betrayal, grief, self-loathing, and stupidity have you on emotional overload.

Listen to the promise we are given in Jeremiah 32:17: "'Ah, Lord GOD! It is you who have made the heavens and the earth by your great power and by your outstretched arm! Nothing is too hard for you.'"

Did you catch that? *Nothing* is too hard for our Lord God.

Jesus is "the light of the world" (John 9:5) and "the light shines in the darkness and the darkness has not overcome it" (John 1:5). In other words, he can handle this, even when—or *especially* when—we can't. By his outstretched arm, he has pulled back the curtain and revealed what you needed to see in your marriage so that he can shine his light into those dark places.

Psalm 139:11–12 assures us that the darkness doesn't have a chance in heaven of overcoming the light: "If I say, 'Surely the darkness shall cover me and the light about me be night,' even the darkness is not dark to you; the night is bright as the day, for darkness is as light with you."

Pay special attention to the last line of that passage. First John 1:5 says, "God is light, and in him is no darkness at all." When we become Light, we are filled with the light. The sinister quality of the darkness no longer has any effect on us.

It's sad but true that sin causes a chain reaction. Your husband's sin may very well have triggered a sin reaction in you. Now that light shines into darkness, shadows of sin are bound to be cast.

What do you suppose might be lurking in the shadows of your heart?

Ephesians 5:13 tells us that "when anything is exposed by the light, it becomes visible." When the light of Christ shines into the shadows, the shadow disappears. God has chosen to reveal to you the truth of your husband's sexual addiction to free you from what was growing in the shadows. One day "night will be no more. [We] will need no light of lamp or sun, for the Lord God will be [our] light" (Revelation 22:5). Hallelujah!

As we wrap up our first day together, I want to encourage you to persevere. You are beginning the journey of healing a broken heart. The two parts of the word "persevere," "per" and "severe," actually mean *through* and *causing great discomfort, damage, or distress*. Press onward despite the discomfort, because at the end of the journey is hope.

What has God revealed to you about your husband's sexual addiction?

Take a moment to thank Christ for shining into the shadows.

Day 2: Needing Hope

I believe God is able to meet my greatest needs as I deal with my husband's addiction to pornography, and that he is in the process of doing that even now, but I'm not sure exactly what that looks like . . . sounds like . . . feels like. Most of the time I feel hopeless and overwhelmed. There are occasions when I feel a glimmer of hope that "better" is possible, but it's rare.

—Amy

"So now faith, hope, and love abide" (1 Corinthians 13:13). If hope is a confident expectation that God will bless you in the future, then you need hope now more than ever. Yet in the early days of discovering your husband's addiction to pornography or masturbation, a sense of hopelessness and abandonment by God may prevail. It feels like the fabric of your life is unraveling and the threads are too knotted up for anyone, including God, to untangle.

Your present circumstances may seem overwhelming. Perhaps your husband has lost his job because of his addiction, your credit cards have been maxed, and your marriage bed has been defiled (Hebrews 13:4). While all may seem hopeless, there is always hope in Jesus. His Word has the power necessary to give you hope.

Match the following verses with their promises of hope:

Romans 5:5	Scripture instructs us so that we will patiently persevere and hold fast to our hope in Christ.
Ephesians 1:18	Trusting the God of hope results in joy and peace.
1 Timothy 1:1	The eyes of our heart must be opened to understand the hope we have in Christ.
Romans 15:4	Christ Jesus is our hope.
Romans 15:13	Hope is not unrealistic optimism; it's the assurance of our future based on God's love.

God isn't about to beat you over the head with a wet noodle for feeling hopeless. It's perfectly normal for you to experience feelings of hopelessness right now. From the very beginning, people have struggled with feeling hopeless.

When everything was hopeless, Abraham believed anyway, deciding to live not on the basis of what he saw he couldn't do but on what God said he would do. And so he was made father of a multitude of peoples. God himself said to him, "You're going to have a big family, Abraham!" (Romans 4:18, *The Message*)

Like Abraham, sometimes we must choose to believe even when there seems to be nothing to believe in, simply because we have hope in God and his promises.

It is amazing to me how God works in my heart and head, even when I doubt I will ever recover from a difficult trial. I have convinced myself that, while coping with my husband's addiction to lust and masturbation, the sun won't shine as brightly as it once did. Then this feeling of brightness sparks in my heart, and I can't help feeling pricks of hope in what I thought was a dead place in my heart.

—Stephanie

The book of Hosea tells the shocking story of Hosea, a prophet who was commanded to marry a known harlot, Gomer. She bore three children. The jury is still out on this one, but the paternity test on these three would not likely point to Hosea as their father. In fact, Gomer pursued love elsewhere and deserted Hosea. Their marriage vows were broken by unfaithfulness, but Hosea didn't seek divorce. He sought reconciliation.

Before we read too far into this story, you must understand that scholars have wrestled with Hosea for generations. One thing is clear: Hosea's life illustrated how difficult it is to love someone who is unfaithful, the way God continued to love Israel. Israel had been unfaithful to God by worshiping other gods. Despite their disloyalty, God longed to take them back, just as Hosea was instructed to take Gomer back. Hosea demonstrates what it looks like to reach out to someone who has strayed even before repentance has occurred. Yet true restoration cannot occur until there is brokenness and repentance.

Consider Hosea 2:2–23, where God confronts the unfaithfulness of Israel, symbolically expressed as a failed marriage. God appeals for repentance and threatens punishment. His judgment was designed to effect restoration. "Therefore I will hedge up her way with thorns, and I will build a wall against her, so that she cannot find her paths" (Hosea 2:6). God's consequences continue, bringing Israel to a point of desperation. When it seems as if the trouble can't get any worse, Israel looks to God and is rewarded with a restored relationship and a promise of better things to come.

I haven't asked you to consider this passage in a secret attempt to advise you either to stay in your marriage *or* to leave. Rather, I want you to glean two important messages from this story.

What does Hosea 2:6 say the Lord will do instead of punishing Israel?

With all your might, pray that the opening for sin in your husband's life would be sealed. Ask God to surround you and your husband with a hedge of protection that is impenetrable by the wicked ways of the world.

Use God's own words to ask him to do that right now.

That's the first point I want you to remember. The second thing I want you to take away from Hosea requires a little background investigation.

Read Joshua 6:17–19:

The city and all that is within it shall be devoted to the LORD for destruction. Only Rahab the prostitute and all who are with her in her house shall live, because she hid the messengers whom we sent. But you, keep yourselves from the things devoted to destruction, lest when you have devoted them you take any of the devoted things and make the camp of Israel a thing for destruction and bring trouble upon it. But all silver and gold, and every vessel of bronze and iron, are holy to the LORD; they shall go into the treasury of the LORD.

What did the Lord command Israel to keep away from (v. 18) in Jericho?

What would happen to the camp of Israel if they didn't obey (vv. 18–19)?

God was quite clear in his command. Everyone in Jericho except Rahab and those in her home was cursed to die, and everything that wouldn't burn was devoted to the Lord's house. Israel was not to lay one finger on anything that was devoted to the Lord. You probably remember how this plays out, don't you?

In Joshua 7, we learn that Achan's fingers itched, and rather than cramming his fists in his pockets, he scratched. Hidden inside his tent was a "beautiful cloak from Shinar, and 200 shekels of silver, and a bar of gold weighing 50 shekels" (Joshua 7:21). As a result of his blatant disobedience, Achan, his wife, his children, his livestock, and all his possessions were taken to the Valley of Achor where they were stoned and God's anger was appeased. "Therefore, to this day the name of that place is called the Valley of Achor" (Joshua 7:26).

In Hosea 2:15 God says, "There I will give her her vineyards and make the Valley of Achor a door of hope." The word "Achor" in Hebrew is `Akowr, meaning "trouble."

The second thing I want you to remember from this allegory in Hosea is that God can and will usher us out of the Valley of Achor to a door of hope. He will transform this place of trouble into a place where Christ reigns with the hope of glory. When the Israelites turned their back on God, choosing idolatry, sexual immorality, and evil hearts, they deserved to be punished. Instead, they experienced the God of hope.

Read the second half of Hosea 2:15 (NASB): "And she will sing there as in the days of her youth, as in the day when she came up from the land of Egypt."

How will God's people respond when he gives them hope in the midst of their trouble?

I have tears in my eyes as I consider the song of exodus I sang when Jesus shined his light into my darkness and rescued me with living hope. He doesn't promise to give you everything you want, but he will most certainly give you everything you need, and whether it feels like it at the moment or not, you will survive. He will deliver you from your trouble.

Close your eyes for a moment and imagine what that deliverance might feel like. Share your song of exodus—your praise for what God will surely do in your life—with him now.

In the story of Jericho, we read that Rahab was delivered because of her courage and faith. To ensure that she and her household would be safe when Jericho was devastated, she was told to hang a red cord from her window.

I know that right now you may feel that there is no one to hold onto. Your husband has betrayed you, and right or wrong, fear of additional repercussions for you and your family may be preventing you from sharing your pain with anyone else. Every day that red cord reminded Rahab of the God she clung to and the fact that he chose to use her to accomplish his will. Jesus is your red cord. Now is the time to cling to him, when you have nothing and no one else to hold onto. He has a purpose for the pain you are experiencing, or he would never have permitted it. He is using your present circumstances to accomplish his will.

One of my favorite Scriptures about this is Romans 8:28: "And we know that for those who love God all things work together for good, for those who are called according to his purpose." If you don't believe this is true, then all the hurt, suffering, anger, and betrayal are for absolutely nothing. I pray that you will believe that *all* of his promises are true for you.

I am well aware that your hopes may have been dashed repeatedly in the past. You have hoped again and again, only to experience disappointment and pain anew. It's tempting to stiff-arm hope in an effort to avoid further heartache.

> I do feel hopeful, but this has been a process. Some days are better than others. Through my Christian walk, I've seen time and time again that it is while in the valley that God can prune me and mold me to be more like him, if I just surrender to him. Sometimes that's easier said than done, but he is a patient, just-in-time God. Every time my husband has had a season of struggling with pornography, he has never lost the desire to have victory over it.
>
> —Nora

I don't want to be the bearer of bad news, but we are talking about addiction here, and the likelihood of recurrence exists. As a result, you can't base your hope on your husband. You will hear me say this many times and in many ways throughout this book, but your hope and happiness must not be dependent on the choices your husband makes every day. "God is faithful" (1 Corinthians 10:13), and that's a promise that will never fail. This journey is a process that requires faithful endurance. It's not a one-time event.

Read 1 Thessalonians 1:2–3: "We give thanks . . . remembering before our God and Father your work of faith and labor of love and steadfastness of hope in our Lord Jesus Christ."

According to this passage, your endurance, patience, and perseverance are inspired by your hope in our Lord Jesus Christ. In what, or whom, are you placing your hope today?

Fill in the following blanks with your first name. This prayer reflects biblical promises God has made to you.

My daughter, _____,
I have heard your prayers and your cry for mercy. I am faithful and righteous, and I will come to your relief. Regardless of how deep your pit of despair, my hand can reach you, _____. I want nothing more than to set your feet on a firm place to stand. Before you were born, I arranged the details of your life, _____, and my plans for you have not changed. Will you trust that whatever I allow in your life has eternal value? I will be your rock of refuge and your firm foundation, _____. Let me be your hope.
Faithful and True Always,
Your Father

Congratulations on completing Day 2.

Day 3: Grieving Losses

After twenty-six years at a very good job, my husband lost his job due to viewing porn on his computer at work. All of a sudden, I was the main breadwinner in our family. It is not a position I ever wanted or dreamed I would have. It took a long time to get past this when it first happened.

—Paige

Definitely trust was lost and had to be rebuilt over the years. There have been times of relapse, which have taught us how to rebuild trust on a continual basis. Initially, I felt like I had lost my husband. I didn't know who he was anymore, and it seemed that the vows we made years before weren't even valid. I had been lied to for so long.

—Jessica

I once had a dream that my heart was made up of little red cubes. One fell to the floor, and I picked it up and carefully slid it back into place. Then two more fell out, followed by another . . . and another. Each time, I picked up the pieces and attempted to reposition them, only to have more fall out. In short order I became frantic, scooping up handfuls of my heart and desperately cramming them into place, only to discover that my entire world was made up of those little cubes, and they were crumbling around me. I was powerless to fix my shattered world.

Don't most of us want a quick fix for the pain we are experiencing? Oh, to have a bandage big enough to cover the emotional wounds and make the excruciating pain fade away! Pain and loss are not things we choose to experience voluntarily. They just happen. And frankly, they happen to all believers. We are assured of this in John 16:33b: "In the world you will have tribulation. But take heart; I have overcome the world."

Bad things happen and we don't get much, if any, say in the matter. Where the choice comes in is what we do with it. We can wrap our arms around the pain and loss and live the rest of our days as victims, or we can discover that God has a purpose for our pain and that he meets us in the middle of it. By choosing the second option, we choose to move into grief, which allows us to heal. Grief is a clotting system that helps a broken heart stop bleeding.

Let each phrase of Ecclesiastes 7:3–4 soak into your heart: "Sorrow is better than laughter, for by sadness of face the heart is made glad. The heart of the wise is in the house of mourning, but the heart of fools is in the house of mirth."

The Hebrew word for "sorrow" in this passage is *ka`ac* (kah-`as), meaning "anger, vexation, provocation, or grief." I imagine all of these feelings are familiar to you. Our *mourning glory* is that by entering into the grief process, our hearts are healed.

Voluntarily entering into grief is a bit like stepping into a river. You don't know how deep the water is, you're not sure about the temperature, and the current makes you nervous. However, there is no way around it; you have to go through it. So, let's hold hands and take that first step.

Now isn't the time to be superwoman and deny your losses, pretending everything is okay and under control when it's not. Until we acknowledge what has been lost in this experience, there is nothing to grieve and no healing can occur. Some of your losses may be obvious (job, finances, health), while others may be less tangible, like trust and self-worth.

Take a moment to identify the losses you have experienced upon learning about your husband's addiction to lust, pornography, and self-gratification. Please refrain from going into problem solving. Now is the time to be real with Jesus. You don't have to put on your "good Christian wife" face.

Name your losses and disappointments.

Ecclesiastes 3 tells us, "For everything there is a season, and a time for every matter under heaven . . . a time to weep, and a time to laugh; a time to mourn, and a time to dance." Now is your time to grieve your losses. If you have held back tears for fear that once they start they won't stop, grab a box of tissues and get on with it. Our God is big enough to handle your every tear. The pain won't kill you, but bottling it up might. Trust me: tears are a language God understands.

> I've learned that you can only praise God to the degree you have lamented.
>
> —Rebecca

Jesus completely understands your grief. Mark 14:34 records that in Gethsemane, Jesus said to Peter, James, and John, "My soul is very sorrowful, even to death." Then he fell to his knees and cried to his Father.

Read Mark 14:36: "And he said, 'Abba, Father, all things are possible for you. Remove this cup from me. Yet not what I will, but what you will.'"

What did Jesus acknowledge or request in Mark 14:36? Mark all that apply:

- ☐ God has the power and might to do everything.
- ☐ Jesus asked God to remove the manner of his death, the cross.
- ☐ Jesus desired the Father's will over his own.

Don't forget that Jesus has firsthand experience with betrayal as well. "Now the betrayer had given them a sign, saying, 'The one I will kiss is the man. Seize him and lead him away under guard.' And when he came, he went up to him at once and said, 'Rabbi!' And he kissed him" (Mark 14:44–45).

I'm certain that, in your heart, you planned the course of your married life to one degree or another. Are you willing to let the Lord determine your steps (Proverbs 16:9)? Will you ask God to help you set aside your agenda and accept the path he has laid out for you at this time? If so, tell him. I'll get you started.

Father, you are a good God, and I fully submit myself to your choices for me, even if they seem painful in light of my preferences. . . .

If you aren't able to pray this way yet, he understands. Tell him that too.

You have probably experienced many losses. Topping your list is probably trust. In the wake of betrayal as a result of a husband's sexual addiction, most wives cite trust as a complete loss. This can feel almost like a death; devastation pierces your soul. You trusted your husband enough to share everything with him—your heart, mind, and body. He was your safe haven, the one whose arms you sought when you felt weak or afraid. Lost trust is such a significant issue that we are going to devote all of Week 3 to understanding how to deal with it.

Numerous women I have talked to have experienced significant financial loss because of their husband's sexual addiction.

My husband ran up a $400 phone bill one month, calling 900-numbers and subscribing to pornographic websites using our dial-up Internet. He also opened credit cards I was unaware of and used them to purchase materials to feed his addiction. It will take years for us to recover from the debt we now face.

—Nicole

Nicole's experience is all too common. When free Internet pornography no longer satisfies their supposed needs, some men expand their repertoire to include subscription pornography, massage parlors, strip clubs, prostitutes, hotel rooms, and travel expenses for clandestine affairs.

Financial loss is compounded when a husband loses his job because of his illicit habits. Not only does this impact the family budget, it devastates the family's reputation as well. Gossip and judgment abound in these situations. Depending on the circumstances and the type of job held by the husband, such information can become public news, creating further pain and loss for the family. Some people will ostracize you unfairly.

Loss of health is also a reality for many women. Nicole's husband's addiction led to extramarital affairs, which resulted in her need to be tested for sexually transmitted diseases as well as HIV/AIDS. In my own experience, the emotional stress from the situation led to severe panic attacks. For a time, thinking about being intimate (even in my second marriage) or leaving my daughter with her father caused my heart to race, fingers and toes to go numb, and my breathing to become erratic. Each time an attack occurred, I believed death to be imminent.

Read Psalm 34:18: "The LORD is near to the brokenhearted and saves the crushed in spirit."

What promise do we find in this psalm even in the midst of our greatest losses? How might you embrace this promise?

It doesn't matter if you've experienced small losses or tremendous ones; they are real and significant in your life. Face them and allow yourself to feel the heartache, knowing that there is One who understands and feels your pain. When Jesus saw Mary and the other Jews grieving the loss of Lazarus, "he was deeply moved in his spirit and greatly troubled" (John 11:33).

Grieving is a process with many faces. Typically, we start off with numbness and denial. It's not uncommon to think, *This can't really be happening. Such things don't happen in Christian homes. Pornography? Not in MY house!*

From there we move into a period of acknowledging the wrong paired with intense, overwhelming emotions like anger, sadness, depression, and guilt. *Could I have done something to prevent this?* It's normal to feel like you're on a wild roller coaster ride at this time. One moment you are heartbroken and in tears; the next instant you find yourself flying into a rage unlike anything you have ever experienced in your life. Some stages will last a long time, while others may barely register as a blip on the radar. Unfortunately, just because you have experienced one stage or emotion doesn't mean you get to check it off and never visit it again. It's very likely that you will revisit some stages and emotions several times.

I wish I could tell you that the journey of a broken heart through grief takes a specific amount of time, but there is no completion date. I'm sorry. But hear this: this journey will not last forever. If you allow yourself to fully enter into the grieving process and wade through the river of suffering, you will eventually climb out on the opposite bank and discover the beauty of a new normal.

Matthew 5:1–4 in *The Message* paints a beautiful picture of Jesus' message to you as you grieve your losses: "You're blessed when you're at the end of your rope. With less of you there is more of God and his rule. You're blessed when you feel you've lost what is most dear to you. Only then can you be embraced by the One most dear to you."

When most people are plunged into grief, it's because of a public loss, like the death of a loved one. Friends and family are fully aware of the cause of their suffering and are able to stand shoulder to shoulder with them. I understand that grief resulting from betrayal is not like that. It's usually very private, covered in secrecy and shame.

Listen to what Ecclesiastes 4:9–10 tells us about sharing the pain: "Two are better than one, because they have a good reward for their toil. For if they fall, one will lift up his fellow. But woe to him who is alone when he falls and has not another to lift him up!"

In the weeks ahead, we'll talk about choosing a safe and healthy support network.

Today I'm giving you an additional homework assignment. I'd like you to begin journaling through your grief. You may use any tablet you have at home or, if you are able, purchase something special to record your journey through the river of grief. I will periodically give you journaling topics. My prayer is that you will begin to recognize God's faithfulness through your losses, that you'll claim his promises as your own, and that you'll seek him as your Source of strength, hope, and comfort.

Day 4: When the Wind Blows

I think God can meet our needs so much more intimately and deeper than we think. It's often, however, not in the *way* we think we need . . . or in the timeline we believe we require. I know there were probably times when I sabotaged "receiving" him and his gifts to me because I was too focused on myself and my husband's secret sin.

—Evelyn

An unknown author wrote about a farmer who was continually seeking hired hands. Because his farm was along the Atlantic seacoast, where storms frequently raged and wreaked havoc on the crops, the farmer had a terrible time finding hired help. At last, a wiry middle-aged man interviewed for a position with the farmer. When asked what his qualifications were, the man responded, "I can sleep when the wind blows."

The farmer found this answer to be odd, but in desperation he hired the man. The farmhand worked hard, and the farmer was quite satisfied with his work. Then one evening the farmer awoke to the howling wind. He sprang out of bed, grabbed his lantern, and raced to the farmhand's sleeping quarters. Panicked, he began calling the man for help, but the man slept too soundly to be roused.

Livid, the farmer threw on his jacket and boots and headed into the storm, prepared to move the livestock to shelter and watch his hay get blown around the countryside by the unforgiving wind. To his surprise, he discovered that the cows were secured in the barn, the chickens were safe in their coops, and his hay was covered with tarps. In that moment, the farmer understood what the farmhand meant when he said, "I can sleep when the wind blows."

When the storms of life strike, can you sleep when the wind blows? Are you prepared spiritually, mentally, and physically for this present storm? As believers in Christ, we can endure the devastation of a husband's sexual betrayal if we have grounded ourselves in the Word of God. It's never too late to batten down the hatches.

I don't know where your husband is in his commitment to work on his sexual addiction. My hope is that he has taken responsibility for his actions, is repentant, and is seeking wise, godly counsel and support to deal with the ramifications of his choices and to make a plan for pure living.

In the context of this book, my prayer is that *you* will also find a safe place to deal with the debris left from the storm. You don't have to completely understand the cause of the storm. Simply trust that *you* didn't cause it. Like any storm, you also can't control it. Now is the time to fix your eyes on the One who calms the storms and stills the raging seas, and find peace in the midst of it all.

Read Mark 4:35–41:

> On that day, when evening had come, he said to [his disciples], "Let us go across to the other side." And leaving the crowd, they took him with them in the boat, just as he was. And other boats were with him. And a great windstorm arose, and the waves were breaking into the boat, so that the boat was already filling. But he was in the stern, asleep on the cushion. And they woke him and said to him, "Teacher, do you not care that we are perishing?"

And he awoke and rebuked the wind and said to the sea, "Peace! Be still!" And the wind ceased and there was a great calm. He said to them, "Why are you so afraid? Have you still no faith?" And they were filled with great fear and said to one another, "Who then is this, that even wind and sea obey him?"

Jesus was calling the disciples to move to the other side (v. 35), away from the crowds in Galilee, in order to reach others. Isn't he usually calling us to the other side as well? Perhaps it's a call to move us away from something—a stronghold, a character issue, an attitude—or maybe it's a call to move us toward something—maturity, wellness, wisdom. Regardless of the purpose, we are usually being called out of our comfort zone into a growth zone.

Do you sense that you are being called to the other side? ___ Yes ___ No

If so, what are you being called to or called away from?

No matter what boat you are in, it's just good sense to have Jesus in there with you. In fact, I suggest that you make him your Captain.

It is striking to me that the disciples seemed unconcerned about Jesus taking a power nap until chaos overwhelmed them (v. 38). Until that point, they were confident in their ability to control the situation themselves. They kicked back, floating along in the Sea of Galilee. Are we much different? I mean, really, aren't we usually fine with what might appear to be God's lack of involvement in our lives until a sudden squall hits? We act as though Christ is simply our dozing copilot, but the minute life presents us with a violent storm, we are screaming in his face to "Wake up!" Like the disciples, we ask, "Do you not care that we are perishing?" (Mark 4:38).

The disciples were freaking out, and for good reason, in my opinion. Storms are scary, and they were human. What are you afraid of? We'll begin next week's focus discussing our fears in depth, but for now, consider some of the feelings that have you tied in knots. Are you afraid that . . .

- being close to your husband will never feel safe again?
- if you let your guard down, recurrence and deception will make you look like a fool?
- you will never feel like you're special to your husband?
- others will find out and judge you and your husband?
- you will be alone?

What if the vigorous winds of the Holy Spirit blow you where you don't want to go? What then?

Regardless of the outcome, you are in the right boat. This boat was constructed to withstand gale force winds and storming seas. Trust that Jesus is your Life Preserver and he is in the boat. He is not sleeping. He is risen! In fact, he is at the helm, so hang on. Pull out a motion sickness bag, because you may encounter rough seas.

I assure you, he is pointing you to the other side, and when the time is right, he will repeat the words of Mark 4:39: "Peace! Be still!"

> I do not know tomorrow's way,
> If dark or bright its hours may be;
> But I know Christ, and come what may,
> I know that He abides with me.
> I do not know what may befall
> Of grief or gladness, peace or pain;
> But I know Christ, and through it all
> I know His presence will sustain.
> —Margaret Clarkson[1]

Clarkson, a poet and hymn writer, knew the Captain of her ship. In her book *Destined for Glory,* she wrote, "Perhaps the greatest good that suffering can work for a believer is to increase the capacity of his soul for God. The greater our need, the greater will be our capacity; the greater our capacity, the greater will be our experience of God. Can any price be too much for such eternal good?"[2]

I would call that "good suffering." Bad suffering results in no change. It's pain for the sake of pain alone. Good suffering, on the other hand, reduces you to a point of being completely ineffective in your own efforts and old patterns of coping and requires dependence on God. Until you experience good suffering, you often do little more than admire God from a distance. Good suffering doesn't mean you curl up in the fetal position and rock away your days. It's anything but passive. Instead, it permits God to do whatever he needs to do with your life in order to achieve his desired and perfect outcome.

When I went through premarital counseling, I remember my pastor drawing a triangle on a piece of paper. He labeled each of the three points with my name, my husband-to-be's name, and God.

Label the following points:

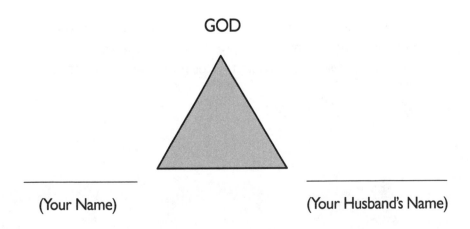

GOD

_____   _____
(Your Name)   (Your Husband's Name)

Then our pastor explained that if we both moved closer to God, without even trying we would also move closer to each other.

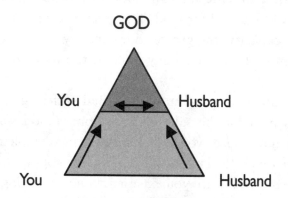

When the thing you desire more than anything else is to be close to God, you won't place demands on your husband to meet your needs. Likewise, when your husband longs to have an intimate relationship with Jesus Christ above anything else, he won't be as apt to feed his spiritual emptiness with pornography. You must not use this information as a weapon with which to hit your husband upside the head. You are only responsible for making sure that your relationship with Jesus is right and is all that he desires it to be.

At the beginning of this section, I asked if you were prepared for this present storm and if you were grounded in the Word.

Read the following passages, which are intended to equip you for this present storm. In the space provided, write the verse(s) in your own words. Make it specific to your personal circumstances.

Psalm 25:4–5

Day 4: When the Wind Blows

Psalm 28:7

Psalm 34:4

Psalm 57:2–3

2 Corinthians 1:5

I hope your greatest longing is to know Jesus more intimately and that you desire to depend fully on him to see you through this storm. One day he will say, "Peace! Be still!" In the meantime, cry out to him, seek wisdom, trust your instincts, and listen to his promptings.

Journal Assignment:

Begin to dialogue with God. First start with: "God, hear me praying . . . ." Tell him all you need today. Then write: "God, I hear you prompting . . . ." Take time to listen, then record the truths he brings to your heart. It doesn't matter if you only write a sentence or two for each starter or if you fill several pages. What's important is that you are making intimacy with the Captain of your boat a priority.

Day 5: Today We Fight!

Until my husband and I attempted to refinance our home, I had no idea about several credit cards he had opened, with charges in the tens of thousands. For years, those bills had been going to a post office box, which was also news to me. My husband worked a lot and traveled often, and I knew something was wrong in our relationship, but I never dreamed he might be addicted to pornography or that his addiction had grown to include paying for sex with prostitutes.

Despite all of this, I know that God is for me. He is all-powerful and able to meet my needs, often before I even know what they are. God can do anything—even repair this marriage.

—Hannah

I grew up in a home where wrestling was extremely popular among the male members of the family. It was rarely safe to sit on the floor to read a book or to stretch out to watch TV. No, putting myself in such a vulnerable position typically resulted in swiftly landing in a headlock, a cradle (which meant my knees were somewhere near my nose), or being pinned on the ground. I learned early that it was best to just go limp and let them pin me (which means they'd conquered their "opponent," in case wrestling jargon is unfamiliar to you). Putting up a fight usually resulted in my getting hurt. I also discovered that when I didn't try to defend myself, they lost interest and moved on to catch another victim unaware.

In Genesis 32:22–31, Jacob engaged in a nightlong wrestling match with God and emerged at daybreak with a wounded hip. At the conclusion of this passage, Jacob was limping on his way to meet his estranged, ungodly twin brother, Esau. Fast-forward a little ways to Genesis 33:4: "But Esau ran to meet him and embraced him and fell on his neck and kissed him, and they wept."

Isn't that just like life? Those who wrestle with God will walk differently, while the godless will run with confidence and strength. Let me tell you something. If your husband is *struggling* with his addiction to lust, pornography, or self-gratification, thank God for doing a spiritual takedown and engaging your man in a life-changing wrestling match with the Almighty. The godless fall, but they don't care enough to wrestle. They go limp. There is no struggle as they excuse their behavior as "normal" according to the world's standards.

The struggle your husband is experiencing is an indication that the Holy Spirit is at work. Praise God! If your husband has never felt conviction for his sexual sin, it may be a strong indication that the Holy Spirit doesn't reside in him. You see, the Holy Spirit *will* do his job.

Second Corinthians 4:17 says, "For this light momentary affliction is preparing for us an eternal weight of glory beyond all comparison."

What does this say about our season of wrestling?

It's not enough to simply pray for your husband during this battle. The Bible instructs us to pray, but that alone won't solve the problems you are facing. You also need to take action.

Day 5: Today We Fight!

There is a great children's story in which all the residents of an island receive their daily meals when the weather delivers it at breakfast, lunch, and dinner. Now that's a great plot for a children's story, but in reality, just because you pray for your daily bread doesn't mean that God is going to have it delivered via an afternoon snowstorm while you do nothing. Similarly, you are to pray for God's strength and protection during this stormy battle, but you also need to get off your duff and fight for your marriage. Follow a biblical game plan. The Restorer will do his part, but he expects you to do yours as well. In the weeks ahead we will talk about several specific things you are responsible for in this battle.

When I was a kid, any time we were playing a game and Dad stepped in to join the fun, everyone wanted him on his or her team. Dad was strong, fast, and cunning—guaranteeing a handy victory. In this battle, the Father is on your side. This battle is his to win.

One of Satan's first lines of attack is often a spirit of hopelessness. This week we have proclaimed the Source of our hope. I pray that you are experiencing a hope that can't be shaken regardless of the enemy's efforts, and a joy that can't be taken despite the pain of your present circumstances. We serve a God of hope, and he is in control. Today we fight!

We find three promises in Psalm 46 that assure us of the Father's *protection*:

> God is our refuge and strength,
> a very present help in trouble.
> Therefore we will not fear though the earth gives way,
> though the mountains be moved into the heart of the sea,
> though its waters roar and foam,
> though the mountains tremble at its swelling.

The Message says that the "Jacob-wrestling God fights for us, GOD-of-Angel-Armies protects us."

Isaiah 43:1–3 says:

> But now thus says the LORD,
>   he who created you, O Jacob,
>   he who formed you, O Israel:
>   "Fear not, for I have redeemed you;
>   I have called you by name, you are mine.
>
>   When you pass through the waters,
>   I will be with you;
>   and through the rivers,
>   they shall not overwhelm you;
>   when you walk through fire
>   you shall not be burned,
>   and the flame shall not consume you.
> For I am the LORD, your God,
>   the Holy One of Israel, your Savior."

See? He is on your team. You are his! In my Bible I have circled the words in verse 1 that say, "You are mine." (You might want to do the same.) Hallelujah—what a Savior! Doesn't that make your spirit want to shout aloud, "Abba, Father, I, _____ (fill in your name), am yours!"

Did you notice all the times Isaiah 43 says "when"? (There are two.) You see, God's Word doesn't say "if" we have trouble he'll be there for us. No, it says "when" you face trials. I'm quite certain that you're facing some of the biggest trials of your life right now. He's got you covered.

How does it make you feel in the pit of your stomach to know that there is a guarantee of trouble ahead?

Day 5: Today We Fight!

How do you feel knowing that you are not alone in this?

Go back to Psalm 46 and read verses 4–7, which promise us God's *presence*:

> There is a river whose streams make glad the city of God,
> the holy habitation of the Most High.
> God is in the midst of her; she shall not be moved;
> God will help her when morning dawns.
> The nations rage, the kingdoms totter;
> he utters his voice, the earth melts.
> The LORD of hosts is with us;
> the God of Jacob is our fortress.

Cities were most apt to come under attack early in the morning, and we are told that God was in the midst of that place at the crack of dawn.

Finally, read verses 8–11:

> Come, behold the works of the LORD,
> how he has brought desolations on the earth.
> He makes wars cease to the end of the earth;
> he breaks the bow and shatters the spear;
> he burns the chariots with fire.
> (verse 10) He says, "Be still, and know that I am God;
> I will be exalted among the nations,
> I will be exalted in the earth!"
> The LORD of hosts is with us;
> the God of Jacob is our fortress.

This is an invitation for you to come and see God's *power* and victory among the nations. God's words in verse 10 should be very familiar to us after yesterday's discussion. However, this time he isn't commanding the raging seas; he's commanding the people.

What might an obedient response to the command "Be still" look like in your life?

The ESV uses the words "Be still!" I also love the NASB translation, "Cease striving." Oh boy, do I know a little about striving! To me, God is saying, "Don't panic. I'm on your team, and don't forget, I'm sovereign." You see, striving is fighting in our own insufficient strength, but we can be still, anxious about nothing, when we know we are fighting with God on our side.

Believe me, just because we have the guarantee that the victory is ours doesn't mean this battle is going to be a walk in the park. Satan will try to thwart your efforts to redefine your marriage in the context of purity and godliness. You will face resistance, but stand firm and take up a fighter's stance.

In the book of Nehemiah, the Persian governors were less than thrilled when Nehemiah oversaw the rebuilding of the wall of Jerusalem. While it seems a bit junior highish, the governors began calling the Jews names and mocking their efforts. When that didn't deter Nehemiah and his building crew, they plotted to attack.

Read Nehemiah 4:13–23:

So in the lowest parts of the space behind the wall, in the open places, I stationed the people by their clans, with their swords, their spears, and their bows. And I looked and arose and said to the nobles and to the officials and to the rest of the people, "Do not be afraid of them. Remember the Lord, who is great and awesome, and fight for your brothers, your sons, your daughters, your wives and your homes."

When our enemies heard that it was known to us and that God had frustrated their plan, we all returned to the wall, each to his work. From that day on, half of my servants worked on construction, and half held the spears, shields, bows, and coats of mail. And the leaders stood behind the whole house of Judah, who were building on the wall. Those who carried burdens were loaded in such a way that each labored on the work with one hand and held his weapon with the other. And each of the builders had his sword strapped at his side while he built. The man who sounded the trumpet was beside me.

And I said to the nobles and to the officials and to the rest of the people, "The work is great and widely spread, and we are separated on the wall, far from one another. In the place where you hear the sound of the trumpet, rally to us there. Our God will fight for us."

So we labored at the work, and half of them held the spears from the break of dawn until the stars came out. I also said to the people at that time, "Let every man and his servant pass the night within Jerusalem, that they may be a guard for us by night and may labor by day." So neither I nor my brothers nor my servants nor the men of the guard who followed me, none of us took off our clothes; each kept his weapon at his right hand.

Which of the following strategies did Nehemiah encourage the people to do?

(a) Post gatekeepers
(b) Post guards 24/7

(c) Carry a weapon in one hand and a tool in the other while building

(d) All of the above

Are you willing to fight to accomplish the victory to which God has called you? Tell him now.

The veil has been lifted and Satan has been exposed as a lying cheat. Yet a war is raging out there and marriage continues to come under fire. Spiritual grenades are tossed into our homes every day by the media. In 2008, the Parents Television Council concluded an in-depth study of prime-time television programming. They reported that across the broadcast networks, "verbal references to non-marital sex outnumbered references to sex in the context of marriage by nearly 3 to 1; and scenes depicting or implying sex between non-married partners outnumbered scenes depicting or implying sex between married partners by a ratio of nearly 4 to 1." If that weren't distressing enough, it has become common practice to glorify "strippers, references to masturbation, pornography, sex toys, and kinky or fetishistic behaviors during prime-time programming on the major broadcast television networks (ABC, CBS, CW, Fox, and NBC)."[1]

If you are ready to take a stand for God in your home, you must commit to relying on God's power, not your own.

Read Ephesians 6:10–13:

Finally, be strong in the Lord and in the strength of his might. Put on the whole armor of God, that you may be able to stand against the schemes of the devil. For we do not wrestle against flesh and blood, but against the rulers, against the authorities, against the cosmic powers over this present darkness, against the spiritual forces of evil in the heavenly places. Therefore take up the whole armor of God, that you may be able to withstand in the evil day, and having done all, to stand firm.

There are some solid promises here for you to hold onto. I want you to make this passage your own. Mark it up and meditate on the instructions Paul gives.

Underline the phrases that tell us what we are to *do*.

Circle the phrases that tell us whom we struggle against.

Put a box around the phrase that tells us *why* we must be ready to fight. Draw big stars around this box—it is important!

I'm acutely aware that your marriage may have moved well past Level I on the sexual addiction scale (see the introduction). As a result, your husband may not be fighting for your marriage. Perhaps he has chosen to leave you and is pursuing his addiction with a vengeance. Please do not feel that you have nothing to fight for. Whether or not there is a marriage left to save, you are fighting for your own health and well-being. You are fighting to not succumb to the slippery slope of sin yourself. Perhaps you are fighting to protect your children from the same enemy that attacked your marriage. You are fighting to keep your eyes fixed on the One who can and will say, "Be still."

My heart feels like it is being squeezed in a vice grip. I so desperately long for you to end this week of reading feeling the strength of the Father as you stand against the sexual addiction that has attacked your family. I pray that you trust and believe that God is your hope. He will comfort you in your grief, and he will be your strength in this battle.

Take a minute to tell the Almighty your greatest needs at this moment.

I hope you know that God has taken up his position on the front line on your behalf. He is able to meet your every need, regardless of the choices your husband makes. Stand firm.

Journal Assignment:

Ask God to teach you how to stand against the enemy and then read Ephesians 6:14–18. In your journal, tell the Father what you will do, in light of what he shows you in Ephesians, as you announce, "Today we fight!"

SURRENDER

WEEK 2

Day 1: Let Go of Being a Pleaser

In my experience, the phrase "I surrender!" often comes with a sense of relief. As a child, it typically meant I'd breathlessly been running or hiding in an intense game of good guys and bad guys with my brothers and neighborhood kids and, frankly, I couldn't take the heat anymore. "I surrender!" was the next best thing to "Olly Olly Oxen Free!"

As an adult, surrender takes on new meaning. It's much more personal. It means letting go of feelings, behaviors, attitudes, beliefs, and occasionally people. On some days the white flag of surrender waves much more enthusiastically than on others. I hate to admit it, but there was a time when my emotional fingers tried to hold onto ownership of my *husband's* daily decision about whether or not he was going to fight the battle of sexual purity.

How I wish I was sitting across from you at a table at Starbucks with nothing but foaming white mocha lattes between us because, to be honest, I can't dance around some difficult issues. There are hard things to be said, and I wish there was a way to look you in the eyes and tell you the truth. So here it is: if you are not willing to surrender things such as being a pleaser, control, fear, guilt, and anger, then you have a faith struggle going on. You and God need to deal with it before any spiritual healing will take place. I'm not going to deny that this may feel brutal, but surrender opens the door for healing.

Read 2 Timothy 2:13: "If we are faithless, he remains faithful—for he cannot deny himself."

The beautiful thing about surrendering is that even when we have difficulty prying our fingers off any one of the five issues we will tackle this week, God will not let go of us. He can't. It's not his nature.

Listen to the comforting words of the Serenity Prayer. You can probably recite the beginning with your eyes closed. The end is far less familiar, but very meaningful.

> God grant me the serenity to accept the things I cannot change;
> Courage to change the things I can; and wisdom to know
>   the difference.
> Living one day at a time;
> Enjoying one moment at a time;
> Accepting hardships as the pathway to peace;
> Taking, as He did, this sinful world as it is, not as I would have it;
> Trusting that He will make all things right if I surrender to
>   His Will;
> That I may be reasonably happy in this life and supremely
>   happy with Him
> Forever in the next.
> Amen.

Did you feel a little catch in your spirit, as I did, when you read "not as *I* would have it"? How about "*if* I surrender to his will"? Ouch. This is about letting go of your own agendas and trusting that God has a plan for you and your husband. In fact, he has a much better plan and a better means of accomplishing it than you could have ever dreamed. I know you are trying to hold on to a variety of things for dear life. Some of them are significant: your marriage, your children, your faith, your mind! But some of them, quite honestly, you need to surrender.

I'm drawn to various images I've seen of a woman standing on a hillside, arms stretched out wide, head thrown back, and hair dancing in the wind. I believe her posture of worship is a physical witness to an inner renouncing of all that has held her captive. This week ask God to help you throw your arms back and surrender! Let's start with your need to please.

> I worked really hard at the beginning of my journey to exercise, eat less, and look my best in hopes of making [my husband] want me again. Although I was a size 0, I still believed I was fat and somehow did not measure up to the world's standards of beauty. I was always comparing myself to other women. I knew that was wrong thinking, and I tried so hard to begin healing that mindset of my distorted self-image, but every time my husband looked at pornography, any ground I had gained was quickly lost. It just confirmed what I had always believed was true—I would never measure up, and I just wasn't enough for my husband to want me and only me. I tried to compensate by controlling my environment—keeping my house perfect and putting things back where they belonged. I lost a lot of joy during this time.
>
> —Jessica

Ask any woman whose husband struggles with addiction to lust and pornography and she will most likely tell you that at one time or another she based her self-worth and happiness on her husband's behaviors, moods, and opinions. It's reasonable for you to feel rejected when your husband prefers to stay up late looking at computer-enhanced images and engaging in self-gratification rather than enjoying real intimacy with you. As women, our tendency is to immediately blame ourselves and then try to fix it. *I must not be beautiful enough . . . thin enough . . . good enough in bed. Maybe if I lose weight . . . fix his favorite food . . . clean the house more thoroughly.* One thing may have nothing to do with the other, yet our compensating behaviors and beliefs increase as we strive to avoid feeling rejected again. Low self-esteem is the natural outcome of being married to someone struggling with this addiction.

About now, I'd encourage you to take a big drink of that latte, and

I'd do the same. Then I'd squeeze your hand and remind you that *you* did nothing to drive your husband to pornography. Remember what the psalmist wrote about the quality of God's craftsmanship in creating you: "For you formed my inward parts; you knitted me together in my mother's womb. I praise you, for I am fearfully and wonderfully made. Wonderful are your works; my soul knows it very well. My frame was not hidden from you, when I was being made in secret" (Psalm 139:13–15). You lack nothing. You are not to blame for your husband's choices, and it is not your responsibility to fix him.

Through my ministry I've talked to women who have agreed to engage in sexual acts that made them uncomfortable because they believed the acts were morally wrong. Their husbands had seen such acts on porn, so the wives had agreed, hoping it would make their husbands happy and want them instead. Other women have agreed to watch porn with their husbands, but rather than having the desired result of satisfying them, it fueled the husbands' lust for greater perversion and polluted the women's minds as well— leaving them with images they couldn't erase.

These are wrong ways to do battle. They are lies from the enemy. You see, we are being deceived by the enemy. He intends for you to be so absorbed in yourself and your feelings of rejection that you will fail to look for truth.

The Gospel of John uses the word *truth* several times.

Read each of the following verses and pay special attention to the word *truth* (italics mine).

- John 1:14: "And the Word became flesh and dwelt among us, and we have seen his glory, glory as of the only Son from the Father, full of grace and *truth*."
- John 8:32: "And you will know the *truth*, and the *truth* will set you free."
- John 14:6: "Jesus said to him, 'I am the way, and the *truth*, and the life. No one comes to the Father except through me.'"

- John 16:13: "When the Spirit of *truth* comes, he will guide you into all the *truth,* for he will not speak on his own authority, but whatever he hears he will speak, and he will declare to you the things that are to come."
- John 17:17: "Sanctify them in the *truth*; your word is *truth*."

Set your latte down, because what I'm about to tell you is significant. The Greek word for "truth" used in each of these texts is *alétheia* (ä-lä'thā-ä), meaning "the unveiled reality."[1] Consider what you learned in the first chapter of this book about the truth that has been unveiled in your marriage. "When anything is exposed by the light, it becomes visible" (Ephesians 5:13). I told you that by his outstretched arm God has pulled back the curtain so he can shine his light into those dark places and reveal what you need to see in your marriage.

You might be surprised to learn that *alétheia* is actually a noun, rather than an adjective. The Truth is the Lord Jesus, Truth incarnate. We can certainly try to battle our feelings of rejection and low self-worth by attempting to please others in ways that exceed human ability, but I guarantee that the father of lies will never stop trying to deceive us. Instead, we need to surrender our people-pleasing habits that focus on our own performance and choose the Truth that will expose Satan's deceptive strategies and point us to a deeper dependence on Christ.

Read Proverbs 31:30: "Charm is deceitful, and beauty is vain, but a woman who fears the LORD is to be praised."

Read 1 Peter 3:3–5: "Do not let your adorning be external—the braiding of hair, and the putting on of gold jewelry, or the clothing that you wear—but let your adorning be the hidden person of the heart with the imperishable beauty of a gentle and quiet spirit, which in God's sight is very precious. For this is how the holy women who hoped in God used to adorn themselves . . . ."

47

What truth does God's Word tell you about lasting, inner beauty?

Let the truth of Psalm 45:11 embrace you: "The king will desire your beauty."

How do these words make you feel?

Constantly thinking negatively about yourself is still thinking constantly about yourself, and that is exactly what the master of deceit wants you to do. Your eyes will be fixed on all the ways you are inadequate and rejected instead of fixed on the Truth. And the truth is that "the King desires your beauty." You are beautiful and sexually competent; you do not need to sacrifice your dignity or make your happiness dependent on your husband's behaviors.

Throw back your arms! Let your focus on your husband's behavior go!

Journal Assignment:

Ask the Father to help you reclaim the woman you were before your husband's addiction began changing how you felt about yourself. Tell him what you will do as you surrender and seek his Truth, instead of depending on your husband's behaviors, moods, or opinions to determine your happiness and self-worth.

Day 2: Let Go of Control

Giving up control is so difficult! I want to MAKE him quit. I want to do it for him. I think if I get angry, or sad, or threaten to leave or whatever, then he will snap to it. It's so hard to admit that it's not about me and there is nothing I can do to control him. (When I try to be supportive, he feels guilty when he fails. When I am angry, he feels like a scolded puppy.) The most difficult part of giving up control, for me, is that I am afraid he will view my lack of comments or involvement as permission to do the bad things. I feel like it's my duty to let him know how he is failing, to keep him from making wrong choices.

—Lisa

Imagine filling a balloon with helium and, with it, all your desires to control your husband and his addiction. You tie a lengthy string to the balloon's knot and then release the balloon into the air— while firmly grasping the string. You send it up in prayer but still clutch the string so you can pull it back down when you want control. You're kidding yourself if you think you've really surrendered control. Until you let go of the string and allow the balloon to float beyond your reach and out of sight, you aren't truly letting it go.

Only when you fully surrender the desire to control your husband and the details about his healing are you demonstrating your trust in God.

God intends to lovingly steer you *and* your husband in the direction of his grace. May I remind you that our Lord doesn't require your assistance? Whether your husband has recognized his need for grace or not, his arrival at grace has nothing to do with you. Your need to control the situation will only act as an obstacle to the work God is doing in your husband's life.

Before you lay a guilt trip on yourself, please understand that having a desire to establish control over something—anything—in a situation that is truly out of your control is normal and to be expected. In other words, you are in good company. Every woman whose husband struggles with lust and pornography has probably attempted at one time or another to regain control in unhealthy ways.

I confess that it's easy to begin to feel like the "porn police." That was the pathetic term I affectionately coined for my need to know details about my husband's addiction. I operated like an undercover detective—wife and mother in the presence of others and super-sleuth every moment I was alone. I spent hours searching the computer for clues about his online choices. I dug through closets, half hoping to find nothing but mismatched socks and half praying I would find the last remnants of his addiction in the form of forgotten magazines or videos.

When I did find evidence of an indiscretion, I would smugly display it where he would be surprised to find it (like in the dining room centerpiece) in order to be rewarded with maximum shock value. I am not proud of this behavior. I hope you will not follow my poor example here, but I never want you to think I'm pointing fingers at your possible unhealthy behavior without fully disclosing my own failures.

You see, acting like a full-fledged member of the porn police never gains the desired results. The behavior turns you into your husband's mother rather than his wife. It communicates a complete lack of trust, which is perhaps justified, but not helpful in the healing process. Most importantly, it only encourages the sexual addict to find ways to be sneakier.

> Early on, I thought my control came in throwing the pornographic magazines out of our home. It gave me a sense of control and power to do something myself to help the situation. Sometimes I would do this and not even tell my husband—he would just find them gone and know that I knew about them. How naïve I was to think that getting rid of the magazines was the cure and made me in control. When I found magazines again, I realized this was beyond my control. And when he said he kept magazines in his office, I realized I could never control this sin for him.
>
> —Nora

Have you found yourself acting like the porn police? We can't begin to eliminate this practice from our daily routine if we don't recognize or admit that we are doing it.

Take a moment to list ways you may have acted like the porn police.

I am not suggesting that you go through life wearing blinders, ignoring obvious signs of a problem and not addressing them. I am suggesting that you don't need to go digging for problems. If you are aware of some of the obvious signs of sexual addiction, you will be more likely to recognize if your husband is in a negative spiral with his addiction. Ask God to clearly bring these issues to light if they exist so you don't need to engage in detective work. Your husband may be struggling with his sexual addiction if

- he is preoccupied with visual sexual images.
- he insists on his own password-protected Internet account and e-mail address, and he won't tell you the passwords.
- there is obvious evidence of pornographic magazines, videos, or computer websites.
- credit card bills show expenses that can't be explained or credit cards that he alone uses.
- he is staying up late after everyone else is in bed.
- evidence comes to light of a post office box where he might receive videos or correspondence from people he meets in chat rooms.
- he is disinterested in intimacy with you but is acting out in any of the ways listed above.

Knowing you have knowledge of your husband's sexual sin, I want to remind you of an imperative we are given in God's Word.

Read 1 Thessalonians 5:11: "Therefore encourage one another and build one another up, just as you are doing."

Given your knowledge of your husband's pornography addiction, how might you be tempted to use that knowledge against him?

How might you apply 1 Thessalonians 5:11 to counteract that temptation?

You could absolutely try to exercise some control in the midst of this crisis either by

(1) using all of the evidence you've collected to humiliate, hurt, or shame your husband,
     or
(2) by extending grace and lovingly encouraging him to imitate Christ's character.

If you were to choose the first option, what would be your motive? Give an honest assessment of how this would contribute to *your* spiritual healing.

If you were to choose the second option, what would be your motive? How would this contribute to *your* spiritual healing? (Don't worry if you aren't sure *how* to extend grace and encourage your husband to imitate Christ's character yet. We'll cover that soon.)

I can't help wondering if your answers are a reflection of what you truly feel and believe or if you wrote what you think the "good Christian wife" answer should be. If I just caught you answering according to the "good Christian wife" rules, rather than because you truly feel that way, it's okay. You may be hoping that your loving actions will lead to loving feelings. This is important though, so listen closely: Whatever you do, always check your motives. "The plans of the heart belong to man, but the answer of the tongue is from the LORD. All the ways of a man are pure in his own eyes, but the LORD weighs the spirit" (Proverbs 16:1–2). And just so you know, choosing punitive behaviors for the sake of reprimanding your husband never works.

> I was very critical and looked at my husband's behavior through a microscope—usually erring on the guilty side. I also used sex as a punishment—controlling when and where it would happen, if at all. If he had been good and behaving, then it was okay to be intimate. If he had messed up, there was no physical touch allowed. I've since learned that this was not the right way to promote healing in our marriage. Boundaries and consequences are so important to healing, but they are very different from punishments.
>
> —Jessica

Let's just cut to the chase here. *You have no control over anyone except yourself.* There it is. You have no control over the choices your husband does or does not make, over his actions, or over his healing. Even though those choices and their consequences directly affect you and your children, you have no control over them. Attempting to imagine all of the "what ifs" will drain you of the energy you need to invest in your own healing.

If you have totally lost it at some point in this situation—ranting, screaming, hitting, throwing things, acting like a lunatic (which is absolutely out of character)—then you know that sometimes you can't even control yourself. I imagine we could swap some stories here, couldn't we? Feeling this out of control is terrifying, isn't it?

I have a strong desire to grab you by the shoulders, look into your eyes, and tell you emphatically that God is still in control. I mean it. God *is* in control. He is sovereign.

Read 1 Chronicles 29:11–12:

> Yours, O Lord, is the greatness and the power and the glory
> and the victory and the majesty, for all that is in the heavens
> and the earth is yours. Yours is the kingdom, O Lord,
> and you are exalted as head over all. Both riches and honor
> come from you, and you rule over all. In your hand are power
>   and might,
> and in your hand it is to make great and to give strength
>   to all.

The psalmist David's life was, as my family likes to put it, drama-ful. He experienced incredible ups and downs, including unbelievable challenges. In this prayer David introduces us to a vital aspect of God's character: his complete sovereignty. You see, God has total control, absolute rule and authority over everything, including you and your husband.

God is omniscient. He knows everything and is able to hear and answer your most pressing questions. He is always intimately involved in the details of your life. Even when he seems far away, his Word assures us that he never stops providing for, protecting, watching over, and caring for you. He knows what you need in this very moment, and he knows what you need in all your tomorrows.

God is omnipotent. His power is unlimited, which means he can handle your husband's addiction to pornography all by himself. According to Romans 8:28, "We know that for those who love God all things work together for good, for those who are called according to his purpose."

What does Romans 8:28 mean for you, especially as it relates to you surrendering control?

God is also omnipresent. He is right there with you. What's more, he isn't going anywhere. "The angel of the LORD encamps around those who fear him, and delivers them" (Psalm 34:7). The fact that you feel as if your life is spinning out of control does not mean God has momentarily checked out to take care of someone else's more pressing need. On the contrary, even though it is hard for you to comprehend, nothing can touch you apart from the permissive will of God. No matter how difficult it is to be walking through this addiction with your husband, your heavenly Father will be with you, working it out for good.

God's plan for you and your marriage is much bigger than you can imagine, and he will work out the details for his kingdom purposes. Your life will never be the same when you begin to comprehend God's sovereignty, his total control of the entire universe, including everything and everyone in it.

Ask God to help you daily surrender the control you long for regarding your husband's addiction. Ask the Lord to help you release your own agenda and expectations into his mighty hand and not reach up to take back the balloon string.

Day 3: Let Go of Fear

What are your greatest fears?

Being close to my husband will never feel safe again, and I'll throw up if he tries to be physically close to me.
   If I let my guard down, he will hurt me again.
   I'll never again feel like I'm special to my husband.

—Audrey

Abandonment.

—Lisa and Nora

Judgment by others.

—Stephanie

My husband will choose to continue in his sin and not seek healing.

—Jessica

Recurrence and deception will leave me looking like a gullible idiot.

—Evelyn

Our hearts will get hardened to sin's deceitfulness again.

—Rebecca

Fear can choke the hope right out of us, leaving us feeling anxious and desperate. We can drive ourselves crazy with endless "what if" scenarios. I imagine some of the fears just listed were familiar to you.

Put a check mark next to the fears just listed that you relate to most.

Name some of the "What if . . . " scenarios that plague you.

Overwhelming feelings of fear cannot be stuffed and ignored. Eventually they will take you captive and result in more pain. God is the answer to a fearful heart. Surrendering your fears to him and asking him to help you work through them is essential to your well-being.

Read Psalm 34:4: "I sought the LORD, and he answered me and delivered me from all my fears."

Read 1 Peter 5:7: "Casting all your anxieties on him, because he cares for you."

These are promises you can take to the bank. There is much information embedded in both verses. Look closely.

According to the two verses, what two things must *you* do?

   1.

   2.

In response to your actions, what two things does *God* promise to do?

   1.

   2.

Why will he do these things?

Fear always sprints beyond our present circumstances to imagine the next disaster that lies ahead. Instinctively, we shut our eyes to block out what we fear most, only to discover that when we open our eyes, we have run headlong into God. Our God loves and cares for us more than we can imagine. When we seek him in prayer and surrender our fears to him, he promises to hear us and answer us. Just as God uses severe physical pain to indicate need for medical attention, he uses fear to get our attention so that we will stop running into the future and instead turn to him in prayer.

Matthew 6:34 clearly tells us not to "be anxious about tomorrow, for tomorrow will be anxious for itself. Sufficient for the day is its own trouble." God will "make straight your paths" (Proverbs 3:6).

Match the following verses with their promise that God's presence fills the here and now:

Joshua 1:9	God takes hold of your right hand and tells you not to fear; he will help you.
Isaiah 41:10	He is always with you; he holds you by your right hand, guides you with his counsel, and will take you into glory.
Isaiah 41:13	God has commanded you to be strong and courageous. He tells you not to be frightened or dismayed, because he is with you wherever you go.
Psalm 73:23–24	God tells you not to fear, for he is with you; do not be dismayed, for he is your God. He will strengthen you and help you; he will uphold you with his righteous right hand.

When your husband turns to images of other women to meet his sexual needs, it is reasonable to expect that you may feel rejected and inadequate, though neither of these feelings reflects how Christ feels about you. It is reasonable for you to be cautious about intimacy with your husband. It's even expected that you may have issues with feelings of failure and abandonment. Fear is what happens when we don't take a close look at these feelings to determine if they are accurate or not. I have heard fear described as False Evidence Appearing Real. This is why it is critical to focus on what is true and real.

Read Philippians 4:8: "Finally, brothers, whatever is true, whatever is honorable, whatever is just, whatever is pure, whatever is lovely, whatever is commendable, if there is any excellence, if there is anything worthy of praise, think about these things."

If you don't get a grip on your fears and settle them once and for all, they will consume you. I know what I'm talking about. If you read the introduction to this book, you know that my first marriage ended in divorce. My husband chose not to take responsibility for his addiction. The behaviors continued and escalated with no signs of repentance or desire for restoration of our relationship. Contrary to everything I believed God wanted for me and my infant daughter, my marriage ended.

After my divorce, fear took me captive. Many of my worst fears seemed to have already come true. Despite God's obvious presence and provision during the darkest days, I chose to fix my eyes on my present circumstances and a lengthy list of "what ifs."

Almost three years after my divorce, I met Mike, who would become my husband. One evening Mike was at our house, and I allowed my thoughts to race ahead to contemplate my next perceived catastrophe. Out of nowhere, fear grabbed me and squeezed my chest like a vise grip. I absolutely could not catch my breath. I felt dizzy, my hands and feet tingled, my heart pounded faster and faster, and I became wild with fear. By this time my fear didn't concern an imaginary future event, but my imminent death. I remember grabbing Mike's arm, gasping, "I can't breathe."

I quickly lay down on the floor with my arms overhead, hoping to fill my lungs with air, but it did no good. *Oh, God! Oh, God! Don't let me die!* I cried to myself. I couldn't imagine what was happening to me.

That's when Mike took me by the shoulders, lifted me off the floor, and in a voice I had never heard him use, ordered, "Walk!"

What? He has to be kidding. I can't breathe and I'm dying and he is telling me to walk? I'm telling you, he was so lucky I couldn't talk because I had several things I might have said to him at that moment! However, because I didn't have the option of arguing with him, I allowed him to take me by the hand and half drag/half walk me around the room. Soon my breathing returned to normal.

Now, it didn't hurt that Mike is an adolescent and child psychotherapist at a world-renowned clinic. He sees countless kids who suffer from anxiety and panic attacks. (Yes, I agree, God has a ridiculous sense of humor.) He knew the classic signs of a panic attack, and I had them all. His order to walk was right on target; the exercise caused my body to begin regulating my breathing.

That panic attack was the direct result of allowing my fears to have power over me. It was the first of many that I experienced in the next six months. I know I am prone to panic attacks, and if I don't trust God with the stressful events in my life, I subject myself to the possibility of future attacks. I would never have chosen to experience the things I did during that season of my life, but I learned valuable grace lessons about God's faithfulness and strength in my weakness that I would never have learned otherwise. God assures us of this when he says, " 'My grace is sufficient for you, for my power is made perfect in weakness.' Therefore [Paul goes on to say] I will boast all the more gladly of my weaknesses, so that the power of Christ may rest upon me" (2 Corinthians 12:9).

God says, "You trust me—period."

There are many reasons to trust God and not fear, but one reason is because God is Love (1 John 4:8). Now stick with my train of thought here. Earlier in this chapter I reminded you not to "be anxious about tomorrow, for tomorrow will be anxious for itself. Sufficient for the day is its own trouble" (Matthew 6:34). You see, Love is so busy taking care of today's business that it has no time to stress about tomorrow. Fear, on the other hand, is so fixed on the potential trials of tomorrow that it fails to address the responsibilities of today.

Read 1 John 4:17–18: "By this is love perfected with us, so that we may have confidence for the day of judgment, because as he is so also are we in this world. There is no fear in love, but perfect love casts out fear."

John is addressing a specific fear of judgment, but I believe he is offering a general principle that can be applied in most instances. This passage tells us that love and fear are mutually exclusive.

"There is no fear in love, but perfect love casts out fear." The only fear we must hold onto is the fear of the Lord (awe and respect for the Holy One), which drives out all other fears.

You demonstrate radical faith when you look your fears square in the face and deny that they have power over you. I watched all three of my children when they were young demonstrate such faith with my husband Mike at the swimming pool. It went something like this: the little one would stand on the edge of the pool, and Mike would hold out his hands and say, "Jump, Daddy will catch you." Now if our children know anything, it's that when something in life is scary, the place they most want to be is in their daddy's arms. I don't think it ever occurred to them to think, *My daddy can't catch me,* or *He won't* really *catch me,* or worse yet, *Daddy's lying. This is a terrible idea and I'm not going to obey him.* No, they recognized that their daddy was in sight and within reach, so they jumped into his arms and he pulled them close. In the process they made him look like the greatest daddy ever.

How might this illustration apply to your current situation?

You glorify God when you trust him to do all he has promised to do. Dealing with the ramifications of your husband's addiction to lust and pornography will test all the coping mechanisms you have to deal with fear. In fact, you may feel those mechanisms failing you. When you experience this, it's an indication that you are in a place where you are meant to grow. Persevere. When you surrender your fears, you will grow spiritually.

I'm reminded of a familiar line from "Amazing Grace": "'Twas grace that taught my heart to fear, and grace my fears relieved." Radical faith that begins with fear will land you in the arms of the Almighty. He is in sight. He is within reach. Jump.

Journal Assignment:

Ask God to bring to mind every fear you have had concerning your husband's addiction. Take as much time as you need to list them in your journal. Finally, ask God to help you surrender the "what ifs" to him. Sit quietly and listen. Write down what he brings to your heart. Is he assuring you that he is within reach? That his ways are greater than your ways? That he is going to accomplish his will through these circumstances? That his grace is sufficient?

Day 4: Let Go of Guilt

"If you didn't always nag . . . . If you weren't so sarcastic . . . . If you loved me, you would do X, Y, Z for me . . . . I wouldn't need to get on the computer if you were more available to me." These are the verses he has sung in the guilt song that rings in my head. I contribute my own verses: If only I were as beautiful as . . . . If I were more capable in bed . . . . If I weren't so critical of him . . . . If I hadn't reacted as I did . . . . The guilt chorus is like a parasite that gnaws away at my rational thoughts. I'm not sure which guilt is justified and which isn't anymore.

—Nicole

Guilt is that sick-to-the-stomach feeling that happens when a chasm separates who we are from who we think we ought to be.

According to the Merriam-Webster dictionary, the first definition of *guilt* is "the state of one who has committed an offense, especially consciously."[1] Now listen to the second definition: "feelings of culpability especially for *imagined* offenses or from a *sense of inadequacy*" (italics mine). It appears that the first type of guilt is warranted. If we intentionally make wrong choices, have reprehensible behavior or unChristlike attitudes, we are guilty of wrongdoing.

65

We should feel regret and repent as a Christ-follower. The second definition, however, implies that perhaps the guilt is unjustified.

When you genuinely screw up, guilt may be justified. Like when your husband's chair was balanced on its back two legs and you put your hand on his shoulder and shoved, causing him to tip over backwards, while you kind of hoped it would cause him a fraction of the pain he'd caused you. (Not that I'm speaking from personal experience or anything.) Yes, that kind of guilt may be warranted, but it need not result in self-condemnation. It should result in repentance and a cleansed conscience. "There is therefore now no condemnation for those who are in Christ Jesus" (Romans 8:1).

Yet self-reproach is almost always our chosen means of handling guilt of any kind, including guilt for "imagined offenses" or those that result from our "sense of inadequacy." Honestly, the fact that you did not lose those last ten pounds after baby number four had nothing to do with your husband's decision to climb out of bed and sneak to the computer at two in the morning. Your jeans size had nothing to do with that. In other words, sometimes we feel guilty for no good reason.

I believe that the most heartbreaking ramification of guilt is that it convinces us that we can't approach God after failing to meet his expectations. It creates a self-defeating barrier to intimacy with our Maker. Oh how he longs for us, but guilt wraps itself around our legs and keeps us at bay.

Guilt also sneaks into a marriage, inhibiting healthy healing. If you think about it, guilt is a very self-centered emotion, putting the focus squarely on you rather than promoting *healthy* concern for your husband and your covenant relationship. No doubt you have asked yourself the question, "Could I have done anything to prevent my husband from choosing pornography?" This is a fair question, but I'm most concerned with how you've chosen to answer it.

Repeat after me (Yes, say it out loud.): "No matter what I've been told or what I've chosen to tell myself in the past, I am not to blame for my husband's addiction to pornography."

If you have to go back and repeat that sentence a hundred times before you believe it, then do it. I'm serious. Some men who are addicted to porn will try to blame their wives for their addiction. That's simply wrong. Each of us bears the responsibility for our own choices. It's as simple as that.

This is when our discussion gets a little sticky, though.

I hate to break it to you, but you have not been the perfect wife. The truth hurts, doesn't it? Before you let this revelation get you all worked up, I want you to know that it was unrealistic to assume that you always *had* to be the perfect wife. There. That feels better, right? However, it doesn't let you off the hook. You still need to do some constructive self-examination to determine if you have done things to contribute to your husband's addiction. (Remember, he is still ultimately responsible for the choices he makes. You are not.)

If you are being honest with yourself, there are certainly things you may have done that contributed to the problem you are dealing with today. Every time you make a decision to act or react to your husband's addiction, you are choosing to feed the problem (pornography addiction) or feed the solution (actions that promote healing). Choices that feed the problem might include, but are not limited to, the following:

- Attempting to control your husband's sexual actions or thoughts
- Withdrawing emotionally (even during times of intimacy with your husband)
- Using sex to manipulate your husband—either withholding or rewarding
- Engaging in sexual activities with your husband that feel shameful or degrading
- Playing detective to entrap your husband with "evidence" of his sin
- Encouraging use of pornography when you don't feel like meeting his needs
- Using past sin against him—revisiting old incidents again and again

- Verbally attacking his manhood, worth, or self-esteem—emasculating him
- Minimizing progress or success as he makes strides in overcoming his addiction

Yes, I know about guilt. I carried it around with me for a very long time regarding my husband's pornography addiction, specifically my unhealthy ways of dealing with it at times. I finally concluded that we all do the best we can and make decisions based on the information we have at the time. Are there things I wish I could take back and do another way? Without question. In my situation, would the outcome have been any different? I doubt it, but only God knows, and only he was able to help me deal with the burden of guilt when I allowed him to have full access to my heart. I'm challenging you to do the same thing now.

Guilt Self-Assessment

Step 1. Read Lamentations 3:40 as a prayer before continuing this exercise.

"Let us test and examine our ways, and return to the LORD!"

Step 2. In the space below, list the things you've said or done that you are ashamed of or wish you could delete or do over—things that have been unhelpful in your husband's healing. List things your husband has suggested you've done or said which have not been helpful in his healing.

-
-
-
-

-

-

-

-

-

Step 3. Pray the following prayer:

"'O God, you know my folly; the wrongs I have done are not hidden from you' (Psalm 69:5). Please clearly show me, of those things I've listed, which are justified guilt and which are not."

Step 4. Go back to your list, and in front of each item, write "Justified" or "Unjustified."

I know that was hard, but may I share a little good news with you? Grace trumps guilt.

God loves you deeply, even when you have really messed up. When you humbly ask him, he will mercifully forgive you for the things you marked as warranted or justified guilt. If you marked something as "unjustified" and the Holy Spirit confirmed that you need to surrender it right now, it's not yours to hold onto any longer.

Consider 1 John 1:9: "If we confess our sins, he is faithful and just to forgive us our sins and to cleanse us from all unrighteousness."

The first time I really understood grace was in college, and I had done something I really regretted in hindsight. I'd blown it, and there was no taking it back. In the face of my overwhelming guilt, I was in a position to finally "get" extravagant grace. As I sat curled up on my dorm-room bed with my Bible in my lap, I realized I desperately needed grace from a God whose love for me was much greater than my sin.

Have you noticed that guilt is a symptom of "rearview mirror" living? Grace is given and experienced in our present circumstances, and faith is future-oriented. That's why Isaiah 43:18–19 tells us, "Remember not the former things, nor consider the things of old. Behold, I am doing a new thing." The Vicki Tiede paraphrase of that passage would be, "Quit looking in the rearview mirror! Check it out! I'm doing something new right here—right now!"

If we look at this passage in context, it's talking about God's mercy in light of Israel's unfaithfulness. Listen to what he says: "Thus says the LORD, *your* Redeemer, the Holy One of Israel: 'For *your* sake I send to Babylon and bring them all down as fugitives . . . in the ships in which they rejoice. I am the LORD, *your* Holy One, the Creator of Israel, *your* King'" (Isaiah 43:14–15, italics mine). Israel's restoration is made personal—intimate.

Your Creator promises, "I will make a way in the wilderness and rivers in the desert" (Isaiah 43:19). Tell him what you long to have restored.

God's intent is not for you to continually look at your past mistakes in order to wallow in guilt and condemnation. He longs for you to honor his present and future trustworthiness by fixing your eyes on him and what he has promised to do.

Read Romans 3:23–24: "For all have sinned and fall short of the glory of God, and are justified by his grace as a gift, through the redemption that is in Christ Jesus."

Do you understand what that means? It means that by his grace, God declares you *not guilty*. When you trust in Jesus Christ, confess your sins, and truly repent of them, *you* (not your past guilt) are justified.

Step 5. If you are tired of rearview-mirror living and long to be part of God's wild rescue, when he will wrench you free from the jaws of guilt, then pray the following prayer:

"Father, as far as the east is from the west, so far will you remove my transgressions from me (Psalm 103:12, author paraphrase). Help me learn from my past sins, so that I might not repeat them. Who is a God like you, pardoning iniquity and passing over transgression for the remnant of his inheritance? You do not retain your anger forever, because you delight in steadfast love. You will again have compassion on me; you will tread my iniquities underfoot. You will cast all my sins into the depths of the sea (Micah 7:18–19 author paraphrase). I will straighten up and raise my head, because my redemption is drawing near (Luke 21:28, author paraphrase)."

Step 6. Turn back to your list under Step 2 and in large, bold letters write *not guilty by reason of grace* on top of everything else you have written!

Grace is free to you, but it is not cheap. It came at great cost. Dietrich Bonhoeffer wrote, "Cheap grace is the preaching of forgiveness without requiring repentance. . . . It is costly [grace] because it costs a man his life, and it is grace because it gives a man the only true life. . . . What has cost God much cannot be cheap for us."[2] We must not minimize the price that was paid to exchange our guilt for grace.

What does grace mean in your life—in your view of yourself and your relationship with your husband?

How does the costliness of God's grace challenge you?

Congratulations! Because you have dealt with any warranted guilt, that guilt is no longer able to sabotage the healing work you need to do in your marriage. I'm not suggesting that this alone is the magic bullet that will make all things right, but it is a step in the right direction. Because guilt is a self-focused emotion, it robs you of the ability to see things objectively from your husband's viewpoint. Stay with me here. *You* need to be okay and right with God, and that has nothing to do with whether or not your husband is okay and right with God. The two need to be separated. You are taking a healthy step toward your healing, regardless of any future choices your husband makes. You can do it. God is your holy destiny. He will help you, so "with confidence draw near to the throne of grace, that [you] may receive mercy and find grace to help in time of need" (Hebrews 4:16).

You have done very hard work in this chapter. Exhale. I know it may have been painful, and you may even feel as though you've bled your way through this chapter on surrendering guilt. Promise me you won't go back and pick at the scab. Though God forgives us, we often struggle to forgive ourselves. Listen to me—don't touch that scab. Forget about it—he has.

> "I, I am he who blots out your transgressions
> for my own sake, and I will not remember your sins."
> (Isaiah 43:25)

Day 5: Let Go of Anger

I listened to his confession and felt sicker and sicker. I was sad and brokenhearted, but in the midst of that a rage, like I have never known, broke loose inside me. I screamed at him, told him I hated him, slapped him, kicked him, called him every nasty thing I could think of . . . and this went on for a couple of months. It turned me into a person I never thought I could be. I would go through stages of packing up all of his stuff and telling him to leave and then, when it looked like he might, I would scream at him not to even think about it. I would tell him he was horrible and worthless, and then comfort him when he got upset. It was completely dysfunctional, and not at all what I had pictured that life as a newlywed would be.

—Lisa

Let's get one thing straight: you have every right to be angry about the betrayal you've experienced as a result of your husband's addiction to porn. Anger itself is not a sin, and I want you to know it's okay to be stinkin' mad! No one, including your husband, should expect you to act like everything is rosy when it's not. I'm afraid many of us have gotten the impression that a "good Christian woman" has it all together all the time and anger has no place in her repertoire of emotions. Wrong!

You're probably thinking, *Hold everything! I see "Anger" as the title of this chapter, and I know we are still dealing with things we need to surrender. Now you're saying it's okay to be angry. Excuse me?*

Anger is a God-given emotion. He wired you to be against things that are evil, but you have a choice: you can deal with your anger in a healthy way, or you can let it consume you. If you've been "playing nice" and kept a smile on your "good-Christian face," then perhaps you've managed not to rock the family boat. However, if your happy face says one thing but your heart burns with thoughts like *If I'm happy, then he's happy, and that's not okay!* then your boat is corroding and eventually you're going to sink. In this situation, all you've done is temporarily preserved a bit of perceived peace in your marriage. You've managed to stuff down your anger, which I'm convinced has yeast-like properties—it feeds itself and grows until you've exchanged anger for rage. In the meantime, you have successfully ensured that positive change will not take place.

On the other end of the spectrum, if you are angry and refuse to deal with it and surrender it (picture the balloon floating out of reach), you're creating an obstacle to healing in your marriage that is as detrimental as your husband's addiction. Sit on that for a minute.

Answer the following questions:

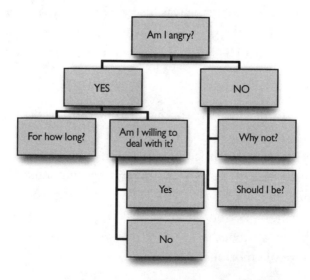

David A. Seamands, author of *Healing for Damaged Emotions,* writes, "The healing process must include the courage to unmask the anger, bring it out before God, and put it on the Cross where it belongs. There will be no healing until it is acknowledged, confronted, and resolved."[1]

Turn in your Bible to Psalm 140 and don't stop reading until you get to the end of Psalm 143. (Do it now. If you say you'll look it up later, you won't. Go.)

That is the dialogue of an angry man (David) with God. Is David desperate? Absolutely. Is he longing for deliverance? Certainly. Overwhelmed? Oh, yes. But notice that David asks God to heap burning coals on the heads of his enemies. He asks God to keep him from speaking, wanting, or doing what is evil. He implores God not to hide his face from him. He sounds like an angry man, don't you think (Psalm 140:9–10; 141:3–4; 143:7)?

As I sat down to work on this chapter, I noticed a date (April 9, 1998) written next to Psalm 142 in my Bible. I was still dealing with fallout from my husband's addiction and my own sense of being angry, powerless, alone, and without refuge, I found solace in David's plaintive prayer.

With my voice I cry out to the LORD;
with my voice I plead for mercy to the LORD.
I pour out my complaint before him; I tell my trouble before him.
When my spirit faints within me, you know my way!
In the path where I walk they have hidden a trap for me.
Look to the right and see: there is none who takes notice of me;
no refuge remains to me; no one cares for my soul.
I cry to you, O LORD; I say, "You are my refuge,
my portion in the land of the living."
Attend to my cry, for I am brought very low!
Deliver me from my persecutors, for they are too strong for me!
Bring me out of prison, that I may give thanks to your name!

The righteous will surround me, for you will deal bountifully
with me.
(Psalm 142)

Pour out your complaint to God. Tell him your trouble. Tell him why
you are angry . . . at your husband . . . at yourself . . . at him.

While there are a multitude of reasons you may be furious with
your husband, it might have come as a surprise that you are angry at
yourself and at God as well. Personally, I was incensed that I had been
so "blind and stupid" not to have realized what was going on. I was
so mad that I didn't listen to my intuition when I suspected that something was amiss. Instead, I convinced myself that I was overreacting. I
also harbored my fair share of anger at God. He knew my desires for
a faithful, loving relationship with my husband in which I was his one
and only and he was mine. Why did God bring me into a marriage
with a man who wasn't able to commit to the same principles?

We know that God himself is "slow to anger" (Exodus 34:6), but
anger that is slow in coming is still anger. There are more than six
hundred references to wrath and anger in the Old Testament, and
it just rolls right over into the New Testament. We read about how
"the anger of the Lord was kindled against" someone (i.e., Numbers
12:9 and Exodus 32:10). God's words in Ezekiel 23:25 are also
indicative of his anger when he says, "I will direct my jealous anger
against you, and they will deal with you in fury. They will cut off
your noses and your ears, and those of you who are left will fall by
the sword. They will take away your sons and daughters, and those

of you who are left will be consumed by fire" (NIV). Forgive me, but I think this gives new meaning to "seeing red." Let's not forget that God's anger was righteous anger against sin; it was always controlled, consistent, and intense.

Read Jonah 4:4 (NASB) and notice what God asks Jonah: "The LORD said, 'Do you have good reason to be angry?'"

How would you answer the same question if God asked you right now?

If you are staring into the face of your husband's addiction to lust and pornography . . . if your heart is in pieces because of betrayal . . . if the marriage vows you made before God seem to have been discarded by your husband, you may answer God's question, "Do you have good reason to be angry?" with a resounding "Yes!"

Here is one of the many differences between God and us. His ways are perfect and ours are not. Many times in the Old Testament we see how he extended his hand of mercy. "The LORD may turn from the fierceness of his anger and show you mercy and have compassion on you and multiply you" (Deuteronomy 13:17). God doesn't always mete out justice the way we would. Mercy, by its very definition, means sparing someone from expected and earned judgment. Unfortunately, we humans tend to inflate our anger rather than our mercy, which often taxis us straight to sin. In other words, we get out of control. I don't doubt this is why Paul warns us in Ephesians 4:26, "Be angry and do not sin." Anger isn't an "if" issue, it's a "when" issue. It's going to happen.

Anger is a directional emotion; it is aimed at someone or something. The term *wrath* usually encompasses revenge or punishment for an offense. If you don't address your anger, wrath usually follows, and when that happens, well, the outcome isn't pretty. We are warned about this in Psalm 37:8: "Refrain from anger, and forsake wrath! Fret not yourself; it tends only to evil." *The Message* says, "Cool your pipes—it only makes things worse."

If you're angry, or if you've been holding onto anger for a long time, you know that it can be a difficult thing to surrender. The problem for me is that my mouth is prone to get in the way. You too? Listen to what Scripture commands us to do.

> Let no corrupting talk come out of your mouths,
> but only such as is good for building up, as fits the occasion,
> that it may give grace to those who hear.
> And do not grieve the Holy Spirit of God,
> by whom you were sealed for the day of redemption.
> Let all bitterness and wrath and anger and clamor and slander
> be put away from you, along with all malice.
> (Ephesians 4:29–31)

This passage carries a punch. Reread it and list the three things we are told to *do*:

1.

2.

3.

Look at these imperatives (commands) and circle the one(s) you think will be the hardest for you to do.

Explain why you circled the one(s) you chose. Ask God to give you the strength to walk in obedience to his command.

What can you do? You can take your anger, which feels like a no-good rock in the pit of your stomach, and use it for a healthy purpose.

Find ways to communicate how you feel honestly and effectively. If your husband has accepted responsibility for his addiction and is remorseful, you may be able to express your anger directly to him. Scripture teaches that there is value in communicating anger if it will lead another person to repent and make changes in their behavior (2 Timothy 4:2). If your husband is not yet taking responsibility for his choices, I strongly urge you to find a support network. We'll talk more about this on Day 3 of Week 3, but for now, let me encourage you to find a woman or a group of women you can trust, or get yourself to a trained counselor. Whatever you do, find a healthy place to be heard as you express your anger.

Let me remind you that God is always available to hear you out. Talk to him. Pray about the situation and your anger before you do something you'll regret.

I also encourage you to journal. Hey, guess what? You're already doing that. Keep it up. Peel back the layers of your anger to discover what other emotions lie underneath. It may not surprise you that anger is usually a secondary emotion, masking other feelings. Think about it. We can often discover those other feelings by filling in the blank: I'm angry because _____. If you wrote "because he betrayed me," the underlying feeling is betrayal. If you wrote "because now our future isn't secure," the underlying feeling is fear. Ask yourself some of the following questions to get to your primary emotions, and journal your responses:

- What is making me feel angry?
- Have I been emotionally wounded—betrayed, devalued, rejected, ignored, blamed, or made to feel inferior?
- Am I making assumptions about the situation or my husband?
- Could I look at this situation differently?
- Do I feel threatened, afraid, or inadequate?

- Am I angry because I have unrealistic expectations of my husband?
- Is there anything *I* can do to change the situation that would lessen my anger?

In your journal, you might write letters to your husband or to those who might have been impacted by or contributed to the addiction. Leave those letters in your journal as a record of your recovery process. Resist the temptation to tear them out and mail them. This is where you are allowed to vent. You can say things you don't have to take back or feel guilty about.

Be mindful of Proverbs 29:11: "A fool gives full vent to his spirit, but a wise man quietly holds it back." You can make your situation much worse if you make rash, emotional, out-of-control decisions. Take a deep breath and refuse to be controlled by your emotions. Instead, practice ways to slow down your reaction. Count to ten before you react to a situation. Speak slowly. Consciously lower your voice—whisper if necessary to keep from raising your voice. Isn't this the exact opposite of what we're inclined to do when we're infuriated? This will take practice.

Finally, base every decision you make on Scripture. Starting now, spend time growing in spiritual maturity. Lifelong learning is a process, but one of the natural outcomes will be more fruit of the Spirit, including self-control (Galatians 5:22–23).

Reading this book is not going to help you "get over" being angry. I'm sorry; I wish it were that easy. However, if you choose to follow the guidance in this chapter, you are choosing to make healthy steps in the right direction. Well done, my friend. Well done.

Journal Assignment:

Throughout the week we have talked about surrendering dependence, control, fear, guilt, and anger. Moving beyond pain and embracing spiritual healing hinge on your decision to acknowledge and let go of these issues once and for all. Do you have unfinished business about any of these issues to take care of with God? Now is the time. I challenge you to make the courageous choice to fill your imaginary helium balloons with each of these issues. Write everything down that you need to release. Tie a knot and tell your heart to "let go."

TRUST

WEEK 3

Day 1: Lies, Lies, and More Lies

Trust was definitely lost and took years to rebuild. There have been times of relapse, and those have taught us how to rebuild trust on a continual basis. Initially, I felt like I had lost my husband. I didn't know who he was anymore. Were the vows we made years before even valid? I had been lied to for so long.

—Jessica

Be·tray·al *n*: the breaking or violation of a presumptive social contract, trust, or confidence that produces moral and psychological conflict within a relationship amongst individuals.[1]

Falling in love is an indescribable feeling. Do you remember when you fell in love with this man you call "husband"? When you stood in front of the minister and made a covenant before God and others to love and honor this man, I'm sure it never occurred to you that giving your heart away to him gave him the ability to break it. While the official definition of *betrayal* describes the breaking of a contract, trust, or confidence, the practical definition should include the breaking of a heart. When your husband's addiction to pornography was revealed, you learned firsthand that the betrayal of love and trust doesn't happen only to other people. It can happen to you.

It *did* happen to you. As you sort through the debris in the aftermath of the discovery, you find your heart lying in the rubble with deep, painful wounds. And you may wonder if you'll ever trust again.

Let's get one thing clear: acting on a pornography addiction constitutes a betrayal. If your husband, well-meaning friend, or a misinformed therapist told you otherwise, he or she is wrong. God designed sexual intimacy to be enjoyed within the covenant of marriage. As soon as sexual pleasure is sought outside the marriage— whether with a partner or in self-gratification while looking at porn—it is adultery. Such choices will devastate trust and have repercussions in the marriage and in the husband's relationship with God. Sexual infidelity is a tremendously difficult betrayal from which to recover, but there is hope.

Did you hear that? *There is hope.* The journey of a broken heart on the road to healing will take time, and broken trust leaves scars. But remember, a broken bone is stronger after it has healed than it was before it was broken. In the same way, in time your heart will heal to be stronger than it would have been if it had never been broken at all, especially if you understand that *time* will not heal your broken heart; *God* will. I know you are up for the journey or you wouldn't still be reading this book. Persevere. In time, you will reach your destination, and God will heal your wounds. "He heals the brokenhearted and binds up their wounds" (Psalm 147:3).

Lies are the backbone that supports an act of betrayal. You have no doubt heard your share of stories. When you asked, "What were you doing up until 2:00 a.m.?" or "Why did you have the office door locked just now?" your husband wouldn't look you in the eye. He gave a vague response, and your trust was damaged. (When I confronted my husband about graphic sexual photographs I'd found in his filing cabinet, he claimed he was doing research for a book. My husband had a very respectable career and was *not* a writer [neither was I at that time in my life], and if he had written a book describing what I saw on those pages, it could have been sold only in an adult bookstore.)

When the full spectrum of the betrayal was revealed, your

damaged trust in your husband was exchanged for full-blown devastation, and you were ushered into the present crisis. Let's consider for a moment what possessed your husband to lie in the first place. I'm going to be honest and give you the bottom line first. Your husband lied *because he could* and because, for a time, it worked. In addition, he lied because he was self-deceived, he hoped to avoid conflict with you, he feared the consequences of you knowing the truth, and he feared the possibility of not being able to "have it all"—you and the outside sexual opportunities. Ultimately, it backfired. As you know, lies are the tool of the devil because they kill trust.

I wonder if, like me, you find yourself creating new categories of time: *before* I knew about the addiction, *during* the unveiling, and *after* the fact.

Name some of the lies you heard *before* full disclosure that damaged your trust.

If you are able, pinpoint the lie that blew the cover off your husband's betrayal and destroyed your trust. This is the moment that marked the start of your "during the unveiling" category.

I know you did not sign up to travel on this road. It stinks. At times, it may even feel unbearable. I recall many nights of crying until I was physically sick. A broken heart is agony.

You don't need to spend much time in your Bible to recognize that God knows precisely how it feels to give his heart to someone, only to have her give her heart to someone or something else. God made a sacred covenant (like marriage) to the people of Israel, and throughout the Old Testament we see them reject him again and again. They committed spiritual adultery, and God was hurt, angry, envious, and betrayed. Does any of this sound familiar? Yes, I thought so.

> Yet he, being compassionate, atoned for their iniquity
> and did not destroy them;
> he restrained his anger often and did not stir up all his wrath.
> He remembered that they were but flesh,
> a wind that passes and comes not again.
> (Psalm 78:38–39)

The real showstopper is that very little has changed in the last four thousand years. The Word of God chronicles a wild rescue story. First, there is a need for rescue (Genesis 1—11), next the rescue is proclaimed (Genesis 12—Malachi), at last the Rescuer arrives (the Gospels), and finally the rescue is fulfilled (Acts—Revelation). You would think we would all bask in our glorious freedom from the chains of the enemy, chains from which the Rescuer saved us. You would think—but that's not the case, is it? Instead, we betray our Rescuer every time we run back to the lies and temporary pleasures with which the enemy tempts us.

Yet despite our repeated betrayals, God stands with his arms outstretched, waiting for us to turn to him so he can forgive us and welcome us back into his arms. God doesn't differentiate between his prodigals. He longs for all of us. Whether we bear the title "betrayer" or "betrayed," God is waiting for us to turn to him so he can begin the relationship again. That's what God does in the face of betrayal. He begins again.

God could choose to grab us under the armpits, pluck us out of our rebellion, and stick us safely back in his arms where we belong. He could, but he wants us to call out and move toward him. He could force the restoration of our relationship, but God allows us to be responsible for our actions. Thus, it is the responsibility of the unfaithful one to own his actions and take the steps to restore trust.

Read Jeremiah 15:18–19: "Why is my pain unceasing, my wound incurable, refusing to be healed? . . . Therefore thus says the LORD: 'If you return, I will restore you.'"

Likewise, you must surrender your attempts to control your husband's life. Let him be responsible for the choices he makes. It is his responsibility to take the first steps to restore trust in your relationship. He will have to earn your trust by demonstrating trustworthy behavior. This isn't going to be a ten-minute tidy. His past lies have probably caused you to question the truth about absolutely everything he says or does, so you can expect that the cleanup from those lies and the rebuilding of trust will take time.

> I am learning that if you still want to maintain the relationship, there must be genuine repentance and changed behavior. Trust, I believe, is earned through a repentant heart, sorrow for the pain you have caused another, and most of all by changed behavior.
> —Sarah

Godly grief produces a repentance that leads to salvation without regret, whereas worldly grief produces death.
(2 Corinthians 7:10)

I don't know where you are in this recovery journey with your broken heart. If you have a strong sense that your husband has not disclosed everything about his addiction and he's still making pro-addiction choices, then trust is not something you can offer him yet. I realize too that you may be someone who has picked up this book after the dissolution of your marriage, and you may never know all the details of his indiscretions. Words can't adequately express how unfair and selfish your husband has been. I'm so sorry! I encourage you to find a group of women or a counselor who can support you through this journey. (See Week 3, Day 3.)

Trust is an asset we don't fully appreciate until we don't have it in a relationship. Before you were aware of your husband's addiction, you may not have given trust a second thought. Since the unveiling, however, you conjure up countless possibilities in your mind every time your husband walks out the door, or you walk out the door leaving him alone, or he gets on the computer, or he pauses while flipping channels, or he . . . You get my drift. It's torture.

Read Psalm 22:4: "In you our fathers trusted; they trusted, and you delivered them."

Read Psalm 25:2: "O my God, in you I trust; Let me not be put to shame."

Circle the word *trust* in each passage.

> Trust is a two-way street. I have to trust that my husband is doing his part in working toward health, and he has to trust that I won't badger him or shame him about it. We have become partners in the recovery time period and both have more wisdom about this addiction.
>
> —Stephanie

You and your husband will not rebuild healthy trust unless you are both sure you are heard, understood, and loved by the other. It is liberating to know you are known and accepted by your partner.

Then and only then can you be who you are—without pretenses. That is what it means to trust.

In each of the passages you just read in Psalms, the Hebrew word for "trust" is *batach* (baw-takh´), meaning "to be bold (confident, secure, sure), to be careless." In other words, trust is when you are secure enough in your relationship that you don't need to edit everything you say and explain everything you do. You can be yourself without fearing that the relationship will end if the other person sees your flaws. This is your goal.

You will choose to trust your husband when you are ready. Don't worry—trusting and forgiving are not the same thing. Rebuilding trust will probably take much longer than it will take to forgive. You will know it's time to trust when your heart helps you choose to believe that he will make the right choices. His behaviors will become your trust barometer. If he wants to demonstrate his trustworthiness and he is making right choices, he will have no problem being accountable and undergoing a reasonable degree of scrutiny. (This does not give you license to be the porn police!) If, however, he insists that you should be able to simply "get over it" and take his word that he's "done doing that," and he resists accountability, you should be cautious about trusting. This is a direct indication that he is not serious about healing from his addiction and restoring trust in your marriage.

Has my husband proven himself to be trustworthy over time? Yes. Do I easily trust him no matter what? Sadly, the answer is still no. I am still very scarred from what happened before, and as a result, I don't automatically trust him. He has earned it, but it is still not easily given. I have to work at it. I have to talk myself into it. Most of the time I am okay, but I do have moments of sheer panic, thinking about what might happen. This is one of the ramifications of what he has done. Sometimes I feel like he has been serving a sentence that goes beyond the crime committed, and sometimes I feel like he's gotten off way too easily.

—Lisa

Name the trust-building behaviors you already see your husband demonstrating, if there are any.

Below is a list of reasonable accountability behaviors you may need from your husband in order for your trust to be rebuilt. Put an X next to the behaviors you need right now. Share those with your husband. Remember that you will rebuild trust in steps, so don't mark everything. Choose four or five for the next month and then revisit the list.[2]

- ☐ Limit overnight travel.
- ☐ Reassure me until I'm able to trust again.
- ☐ Be transparent; share your intimate thoughts and feelings with me.
- ☐ Share your positive feelings about me.
- ☐ Tell me what you need from me.
- ☐ Spend time connecting with me (spiritually, emotionally, physically, and sexually).
- ☐ Tell me what upset you during the day.
- ☐ Listen to my positive and negative feelings, and don't try to "fix" things.
- ☐ Focus on what I'm saying and don't be distracted when we talk.
- ☐ Show me affection outside the bedroom.
- ☐ Hold me and show understanding when I'm upset; don't give up on me.
- ☐ Avoid old patterns that are a temptation.

☐ Resist the temptation to pressure me to heal faster.

☐ Make your cell phone, bank statements, credit card statements, and e-mail accounts available to me.

☐ Get into couples therapy and/or individual therapy with me and work to figure out exactly what the betrayal says about you, me, and us.

☐ Offer full disclosure—tell me the whole truth.

☐ Tell me when you are tempted to relapse.

I can't promise you that this will be an easy road to travel. Nor can I assure you that if you arrive at your destination and choose to trust, your husband will not fall again. But I can tell you that God will heal your broken heart.

It's no longer about "Will David re-offend?" I'm pretty sure he might. It's about the quality of the relationship that we maintain, whether or not he's perfect. It's about whether or not we've got each other's back. I would rather know he's got my back and I've got his than that he or I have to be perfect. It's about the safe harbor that exists between us . . . despite the size of the hurricane that hits our house.

—Olivia

Day 2: Well-Placed Trust

I had to go beyond the idea of trusting my husband to the root of "Do I trust God?" I wrestled with the truth that "God works for the good of those who love him" and that his plan was "to prosper [me] not to harm [me]." This *thing* seemed very evil to me, and I did not want it as part of our lives, but here it was. I took my questions to God and at times yelled at him for allowing this addiction. I realized God could handle my doubts and my questions. His love for me would never fail, and he could handle anything I threw at him. I journeyed to the place where I learned to trust God even though I did not *feel* like I could trust my husband. I had to trust God to lead, teach, correct, discipline, and heal my husband.

—Melissa

I used to lie in bed and mentally recount every conversation with my husband, every action and reaction he had as well as his body language. I attempted to peel back the layers of what was said or done to discover the true intent or the lies that might lurk beneath the surface. I had placed a high degree of trust in that man on the day we said "I do," and I learned the hard way that this trust was misplaced. I had been deceived, and I felt like a fool. How could I have been so blind? How could I have missed what now, in hindsight, seemed like a neon sign flashing "Warning! Warning! Something is wrong here!"?

God met me in my deep pit of despair. As I staggered around with a bleeding heart and deep emotional wounds, God the Healer took my heart and bound it in his mercy. He reminded me that he only gives what is good. His endless love and inability to lie eclipsed the pain in my heart. I surrendered to the One who was and is and always will be. I chose to trust the One who chose to give his life for me. It was well-placed trust. It became clear that I should never have given another human being the level of trust that must be reserved for God alone. (Not that I should never trust another human being, but I should not give the "sold out" trust I had for my Savior.) In that sweet spot of unabashed trust, I longed for more of God. He filled the gashes and fractures in my heart and began to heal me.

> Trust in the LORD with all your heart,
> and do not lean on your own understanding.
> In all your ways acknowledge him,
> and he will make straight your paths.
> (Proverbs 3:5–6)

I want you to be fully equipped to rebuild healthy trust with your eyes wide open. Many times in the writing of this book I have taken my fingers off the keys and gone facedown on the floor to cry out to *Abba* on your behalf. I have prayed for each woman who reads these words to be set free from suffocating anguish and dread of the future, knowing that she will be all right regardless of her husband's choices because God "will make straight [her] paths."

He is God.

Your husband is not.

Let that sink in.

Day 2: Well-Placed Trust

Helen Keller wrote the following:

> Four things to learn in life:
> To think clearly without hurry or confusion;
> To love everybody sincerely;
> To act in everything with the highest motives;
> To trust God unhesitatingly.[1]

What might each of these lessons look like in the context of your marriage? Let's take them one at a time.

"To think clearly without hurry or confusion" would mean I . . .

"To love everybody sincerely" would mean I . . .

"To act in everything with the highest motives" would mean I . . .

"To trust God unhesitatingly" would mean I . . .

Don't you think that one reason we have a hard time trusting God is because his ways sometimes don't make sense to us? Let's be honest. He asked Noah to build an ark before it had ever rained on the earth, and according to some theologians, it might have taken the man a hundred years to build the boat! This does not seem like the most efficient plan. I'm not questioning him; I'm just saying that at first glance, you can't really point fingers at Abram (Abraham) and Sarai (Sarah) when they went ahead of God and tried to "help" him fulfill his promise to make them a "great nation" (Genesis 15–17). Consider the facts.

Look at Genesis 12:4. How old was Abram when he received God's promise to make him into a "great nation"? If you were Abram, when would you expect God to fulfill his promise?

Read Genesis 17:15–17. How old was Abraham when the promise was finally fulfilled? Do the math. How many years had passed?

Turn to Hebrews 11:11–12. By what means did Abraham, who was "as good as dead," see his delayed promise fulfilled? What does that say to you?

Are you willing to wait on God's timetable in your life? Do you have a tendency to run ahead of him and try to help him along? It's especially hard to surrender to God's will when it also means abiding by his time frame. I know what I want, and I wanted it yesterday. Yet often it seems God will wait. He will wait as long as it takes for us to exhaust our human efforts, put total trust in him, surrender our will, and expect the impossible from the Creator of possibilities. I think this is why God assured the Israelites on the bank of the Red Sea as he did: "Fear not, stand firm, and see the salvation of the LORD, which he will work for you today . . . . The LORD will fight for you, and you only have to be silent" (Exodus 14:13–14).

> For the LORD is good; his steadfast love endures forever,
> and his faithfulness to all generations. (Psalm 100:5)

When you accepted the gift of salvation from Jesus, your name was written in the Book of Life. From that moment on you began an uphill journey of faith with the "Author of life" (Acts 3:15) to your final destination. Sentence after sentence you climbed, growing in your faith. Then suddenly you encountered parentheses— things that altered the flow of your life as something unexpected was inserted. After walking in on a scene you never dreamt of, hearing a tearful confession, or perhaps discovering an unexplained bill, you found yourself in a place you didn't expect to be and hadn't anticipated. You learned of your husband's addiction to lust and pornography, and you found yourself living in parentheses.

Sometimes you wonder if God is going to show up for the wild rescue or if he is going to leave you there indefinitely. The biggest mistake you can make is to believe that God has grown bored looking out for you and has shifted his attention to a Christian who is more appreciative and consistent in her faith. He is not leaving you to fend for yourself.

What evidence have you seen, heard, or experienced that God has not abandoned you? Was it answered prayer? A word of encouragement? A promise in his Word?

When you are waiting in the parentheses between "what was" and "what will be," you are living before the face of God. You are living *coram Deo*. This parenthetical moment will require you to have unwavering trust in the sovereignty of God. Though your circumstances may not change, your ability to trust God is strengthened through a keen sense of his presence *in* the parentheses. The Bible explains: "Now faith is the assurance of things hoped for, the conviction of things not seen"(Hebrews 11:1).

If you found it challenging to think of ways you have experienced God in the middle of your trial, then, like me, you are probably prone to becoming so preoccupied with the pressing details of your situation that you fail to see his providential care for you. Stop. Enter into his rest.

Read Deuteronomy 33:12: "The beloved of the LORD dwells in safety. The High God surrounds him all day long, And dwells between his shoulders."

Can you picture it? You, his beloved child, resting between the curve of his shoulders. (Do you see the curve of your parentheses?) Do you get chills thinking about how precious it is to know you can rest safely in his divine presence? Listen carefully . . . between his shoulders you will find his heart.

As we continue our ascent to the throne of God, we need to keep looking up. Then, when we are at our wit's end and our eyes are fixed on him, we will have a clear perception of him at work.

Day 2: Well-Placed Trust

Read the last sentence of 2 Chronicles 20:12 in your Bible. Record Jehoshaphat's words here.

> I asked God to show me *trust* in his Word, and he did.
>
> —Amy

Where you look will determine what you believe, which will impact what you expect God to do. Faith trusts God for all he promises. Sometimes, before you see the tangible evidence of his work, all you have is faith in his Word. If he says it, he will do it. You can take that to the bank.

You can learn to trust God by seeking passages that assure you he is trustworthy. Then ask him to calibrate your heart and your thoughts so that they are in alignment with his Word. Own those new thoughts, and then regulate your behaviors to match them.

Believing that God will do what he has promised *before* you see him do it glorifies him as you honor his present and future trustworthiness. You can trust the Man who died for you.

Journal Assignment:

Copy the following verses into your journal. They assure you of God's trustworthiness. Write them on sticky notes and tack them around the house. Write them on index cards and put them on a ring. Keep it where you can flip through them often. Own these verses. In your journal, ask God to transform your heart and mind and align your actions to match your new thoughts.

Commit your way to the LORD; trust in him and he will act.
He will bring forth your righteousness as the light,
and your justice as the noonday. (Psalm 37:5–6)

(continues)

"I know that you can do all things and that no purpose of yours can be thwarted." (Job 42:2)

Thus says the LORD . . . "Blessed is the man who trusts in the LORD,
whose trust is the LORD.
He is like a tree planted by water,
that sends out its roots by the stream,
and does not fear when heat comes,
for its leaves remain green,
and is not anxious in the year of drought,
for it does not cease to bear fruit."
(Jeremiah 17:7–8)

So we do not lose heart.
Though our outer self is wasting away,
our inner nature is being renewed day by day.
For this light momentary affliction is preparing for us
an eternal weight of glory beyond all comparison,
as we look not to the things that are seen
but to the things that are unseen.
For the things that are seen are transient,
but the things that are unseen are eternal.
(2 Corinthians 4:16–18)

Day 3: Safe Support

I told my closest childhood friend first, and she ended up sharing her story as well. Then I found a small group of women who were also dealing with their husband's addictions, and we have journeyed together for years now. We stopped meeting regularly about two years after our husbands' addictions were made known, but we still meet several times a year to visit, talk, and check in on one another. I also know that they would be there if I needed them. We did tell our families about two years after, when we renewed our marriage vows.

—Melissa

I gave my testimony to my MOPS group steering committee one year. We were taking turns giving our testimonies. I was really nervous, but felt it was something I was supposed to do. I put it off until the last meeting of the year. I couldn't give an accurate picture of what Jesus had done in my life without mentioning the difficult times I had been through with my husband. I'll just say that my testimony was beyond what anyone else shared. After I was done, some ladies wiped tears from their eyes while the group coordinator simply said, "Okay . . . well . . ." and stammered around a bit. I actually thought it was pretty funny. It was really liberating, and I knew this was a group of trustworthy women. Even though none of them told me they were in a similar situation, just saying the words out loud to these women had a great impact on my recovery. It made it less of a "dirty little secret."

—Dianna

Have you heard of the "20/50 Crisis"[1]? It's based on the staggering statistic that 20 percent of Christian women and 50 percent of Christian men are addicted to pornography. You'd never know it to look around the church though, would you?

When I was in college, I had the opportunity to study overseas. One of the highlights of the trip was seeing *Phantom of the Opera* at Her Majesty's Theatre in London. Many years later (we aren't saying *how* many!), one song in particular still haunts me, especially when I look around the church. "Masquerade!" makes the point that everywhere you look you see a parade of masks disguising a person's true self from the world.

If in fact 50 percent of Christian men struggle with pornography, then it is quite likely (assuming many of them are married and their wives know about the addiction) that up to 50 percent of the Christian women in a given church are hiding behind their "Everything's fine" mask. Healing's greatest enemy is silence. The following story is a case in point.

Read the story of Tamar (2 Samuel 13:1–14):

Now Absalom, David's son, had a beautiful sister, whose name was Tamar. And after a time Amnon, David's son, loved her. And Amnon was so tormented that he made himself ill because of his sister Tamar, for she was a virgin, and it seemed impossible to Amnon to do anything to her. But Amnon had a friend, whose name was Jonadab, the son of Shimeah, David's brother. And Jonadab was a very crafty man. And he said to him, "O son of the king, why are you so haggard morning after morning? Will you not tell me?" Amnon said to him, "I love Tamar, my brother Absalom's sister." Jonadab said to him, "Lie down on your bed and pretend to be ill. And when your father comes to see you, say to him, 'Let my sister Tamar come and give me bread to eat, and prepare the food in my sight, that I may see her and eat it from her hand.'" So Amnon lay down and pretended to be ill. And when the king came to see him, Amnon said to the king, "Please let my sister Tamar come and make a couple of cakes in my sight, that I may eat from her hand."

Then David sent home to Tamar saying, "Go to your brother Amnon's house and prepare food for him." So Tamar went to her brother Amnon's house, where he was lying down. And she took dough and kneaded it and made cakes in his sight and baked the cakes. And she took the pan and emptied it out before him, but he refused to eat. And Amnon said, "Send out everyone from me." So everyone went out from him. Then Amnon said to Tamar, "Bring the food into the chamber, that I may eat from your hand." And Tamar took the cakes she had made and brought them into the chamber to Amnon her brother. But when she brought them near him to eat, he took hold of her and said to her, "Come, lie with me, my sister." She answered him, "No, my brother, do not violate me, for such a thing is not done in Israel; do not do this outrageous thing. As for me, where could I carry my shame? And as for you, you would be as one of the outrageous fools in Israel. Now therefore, please speak to the king, for he will not withhold me from you." But he would not listen to her, and being stronger than she, he violated her and lay with her.

There are no specific examples of pornography in the Bible, but there are numerous examples of biblical men who struggled with lust and sin, and many of them were married. Unfortunately, the Bible is silent on how the wives dealt with their husband's sin. In the story of Tamar's rape, however, we get a sneak peek at a man who was consumed by lust to the point of betraying the one he professed to love.

How is Amnon's behavior similar to a man who is addicted to lust, masturbation, or pornography?

Compare Jonadab's influence and encouragement to the messages men get from today's media, fashion, advertisers, and societal influences.

What feelings were evoked when you heard Tamar's plea, "As for me, where could I carry my shame?"

In what ways does a woman betrayed by a husband's addiction bear the stigma of shame?

Now read the outrageous counsel Tamar receives in
2 Samuel 13:20:

> And her brother Absalom said to her, "Has Amnon your brother
> been with you? *Now hold your peace,* my sister. He is your
> brother; *do not take this to heart.*" So Tamar lived, a desolate
> woman, in her brother Absalom's house. (italics mine)

Before we are too hard on Absalom, we should acknowledge that
his words were probably a lame attempt to offer comfort to his sister, who was undoubtedly in shock. He was horrified by the cultural
implications of what had just happened. Nonetheless, Absalom's
words cut to the heart, don't they? "Now hold your peace . . . . Do
not take this to heart." You may not have heard those exact words,
but I imagine you have heard similar utterances. You may have even
said them to yourself a time or two. I'm convinced that the deceiver
fastens himself to us like a clip-on earring and whispers lies in our
ears all through the day and night. He tells us to stuff the painful
emotions and to keep our family's "dirty little secret" hidden.

According to 2 Samuel 13:20 (which you just read), how was
Tamar described as she lived with her brother?

The Hebrew word for "desolate" is *Shamem* (shaw-mame´),
meaning to be devastated, ravaged, deflowered, and appalled. While
there seems to be no obvious linguistic connection between the two,
I'm struck by how much *Shamem* looks and sounds like *shame*.
Desolation is no way for a woman to live her life, but the ramifications of "keeping quiet" and burying feelings will not contribute to
your spiritual healing. It will only exacerbate your undeserved sense
of shame. Scripture gives us clear evidence of what happens when
we don't talk to someone about what's going on in our life.

Read Psalm 39:1–4:

> I said, "I will guard my ways, that I may not sin with my tongue;
> I will guard my mouth with a muzzle,
> so long as the wicked are in my presence."
> I was mute and silent, I held my peace to no avail,
> and my distress grew worse.
> My heart became hot within me.
> As I mused, the fire burned;
> then I spoke with my tongue:
> "O LORD, make me know my end
> and what is the measure of my days;
> let me know how fleeting I am!"

When the psalmist's heart grew hot and he finally broke his silence, to whom did he speak?

It is essential that you find some people to talk to, and the first person should be God. The most important thing you can do is pray. I'm not talking about proper "good church lady" praying. I'm talking about facedown, pour-your-heart-out, surrender-all, yell, cry, and praise-him praying. This is the time to be more honest and transparent with God than ever before. Then ask him to direct your ways, specifically directing you to a safe person to talk to.

This is not news you want broadcasted. I get that. While you need to talk to others, you must not throw it out there to every person you see. There can be unpleasant repercussions if you do not exercise caution and discernment here.

> "Fear not. These are the things that you shall do: Speak the truth
> to one another; render in your gates judgments that are true and
> make for peace." (Zechariah 8:15–16)

Before I give you some do's and don'ts about finding safe confidants, I need you to understand something important. There are only two kinds of experiences for women in your situation. There is *your* experience, and there is *everyone else's* experience. No one else's experience will be exactly like yours. Period. No one else has the exact same family of origin, life experiences, temperament, husband, or circumstances. There are no cookie-cutter experiences, so you may read something and think, *I know for a fact that this would not be the case with my parents, friends, or pastor.* What I'm about to share with you is "best practice" counsel. In the majority of cases, everything I'm about to describe for you is true. But this is *your* experience. If you are like me, you may not make the best decisions when you are in crisis. If you choose not to listen to me, please promise me you will pray long and hard before you do anything rash.

If your husband is committed to restoring your marriage and he is taking obvious steps in the right direction, I strongly encourage you to consult him about who and how much to tell. You both need a support group right now. Take time to pray together about those you might include.

Your best confidants will be those who are equipped to listen without judgment. You don't need someone who will attempt to fix it for you. Ideally, you want to talk to someone who can share her own experiences of betrayal and is now walking in victory.

Your first inclination might be to run to family. That was my first response. Thankfully, the Holy Spirit held me back. I can only give him credit because I wasn't talking to anyone else and no one suggested that I think twice about telling my parents immediately. I knew beyond a shadow of a doubt that if my daddy knew the truth, he would come riding halfway across the country on a big ol' horse and rescue me from the hell in which I was living. Never would he allow me to feel the hurt I was feeling if he could do anything about it.

But I came to the conclusion that, as long as there was any hope in my heart that my marriage could be restored, it was prudent not to tell my family. Their desire to protect me would create an obstacle to any recovery process I might go through with my husband. Likewise, if my marriage was restored, I could never take back the words I had already shared with them about my husband. While my husband and I would have gone through the painful process of healing, my family would not have experienced the restoration in the same way. When the time was right, I eventually told my family as much of the story as they needed to know. There are just some things you don't need your family to know, if you know what I mean.

My second instinct was to go to the church. If we are seeking spiritual healing and our marriage is in crisis, it makes sense to go to the place where we were married. Listen to me carefully. I love the local church, and I feel very strongly about submitting to the authority of a healthy local church (emphasis on *healthy*). I do not attend your church, so I can't tell you with certainty whether your church is the place to go for help or not. However, I encourage you to proceed with prayerful caution. It pains me to give this warning, but not all churches and pastors are safe places. I've heard too many stories of wounded women going to their church after learning about their husband's addiction, and receiving counsel that does not promote healing. (See appendix B.)

Pastors are human, and they may or may not be equipped to counsel a woman in your situation. Some pastors may be tempted to spiritualize the pain. For instance, this is not a time when you want your husband's addiction to be rationalized with the verse "No temptation has overtaken [him] that is not common to man" (1 Corinthians 10:13). Likewise, you don't want your pain explained away with "All who desire to live a godly life in Christ Jesus will be persecuted" (2 Timothy 3:12). Though perhaps well intentioned, spiritual platitudes and simplistic pietism would not be helpful. Other pastors may be exceptionally well trained in this area and enormously helpful. (But be warned, you may not like what they have to say. Sometimes the truth hurts. Sorry.)

During the Reformation, Luther and Calvin established "marks" of the church. These characteristics distinguished a true church from a false church. I believe these are still true today. As you consider whether your church is a safe place to share your problem, let's start there. The "marks" of a true church are that they preach the Word of God, including the gospel message of salvation by faith in Christ alone, and they include the administration of the sacraments (baptism and the Lord's Supper). I would add the following indicators. How does your church measure up?

- Is it a place of joy?
- Do you see God at work?
- Do you see evidence that people genuinely care for and pray for each other?
- Are you made to feel like a member of the family?
- Are you aware of other difficult issues that have been brought to leadership? How were they received and handled?

In addition to evaluating whether your church is a safe place to go for help, I also strongly encourage you to get yourself to a professional counselor. I would be remiss if I didn't tell you that you need help from someone trained to deal with these issues. Appendix A lists a variety of resources for finding professional therapists who deal with sex addictions and the wives of sex addicts. Not just any therapist will do, and a good one will tell you if he or she is qualified to help you. Call and ask questions. Find out if they see women like you. Do they promote individual as well as couples therapy? Are they familiar with the professionals who are considered experts in this area (Dr. Mark Laaser, Dr. Patrick Carnes, Dr. Drew Carder, and Dr. Harry Schaumburg)? If they are not qualified to help you, they will likely refer you to someone who is. Do not be discouraged; just call the next person.

A counselor may be your best resource for a support group. Trust me when I tell you that you cannot put a price tag on a solid support group. Here's why. First of all, the women in the group have all been in your shoes. While reading this book, you have probably thought, *How did Vicki know this is exactly how I feel?* For the same reason, the women in your support group will encourage you and empathize while maintaining confidentiality.

Not all support groups look the same. Some are facilitated by a therapist, some are led by lay leaders, and others may be in a church or home and led by another wife navigating her way through her own journey of a broken heart. Each offers a different atmosphere. A support group should be a safe place to be yourself and feel accepted. No one is there to judge you. Their primary objective should not be to fix you or tell you what to do. Rather, they will respectfully listen (and you'll listen to them), they'll point you to Christ, they'll objectively present options for you to consider, and they'll be your friends. Best of all, women in your support group will allow you to be angry, cry, and walk through each stage of grieving while taking you by the shoulders when necessary and saying, "Friend, what are you thinking?"

You may have a close personal girlfriend or two with whom you can confide. After prayer, you may decide it's safe to share with them. Be aware, however, that if they have never been in your position, they may inadvertently become one of Job's comforters. (If you recall, Job was a faithful, righteous man who lost his family and property. Job had three friends who meant to comfort Job but succeeded only in discouraging and finding fault.) A girlfriend who hasn't walked in your shoes may mean well, but she may not realize how unhelpful or hurtful her words may be. You can't expect her to know what it's like to be the wife of a porn addict if she's never been one. Therefore, you can't expect her to have the words to comfort you. Like your family, your girlfriends won't be on the road to recovery with you and your husband. Whatever you say to them will stick, and there's no taking anything back once the words are said.

Tamar did not have the options you have. She kept quiet, but she paid the price because she couldn't help but "take it to heart," and the results were devastating. Pray. Ask God to direct you to safe support.

> "Ah, Lord GOD! It is you who have made
> the heavens and the earth by your great power
> and by your outstretched arm!
> Nothing is too hard for you."
> (Jeremiah 32:17)

I encourage you to pray the following prayer:

Heavenly Father, surely you are present here. I long to be drawn into your embrace, and I'm so thankful that none of the feelings I share with you are too much for you to handle. Direct me to those with whom you would have me share my story so that they might be a source of encouragement and guidance on this journey of healing. You are sovereign, and I trust that you will carry me to places where my own feet could never take me. My hope is in you, as you take this unplanned, unwelcomed journey through addiction with me. I know I am not alone. I lay my husband at your feet and place my heart in your hands. May your will be done. In the name of your Son, Jesus Christ my Lord, Amen.

Day 4: Intimacy

We were encouraged by our counselor to go on a sexual fast for forty days. It offered me a period of time to feel safe and not deal with how to say no to him until we had some time to deal with the issue. Our fast lasted longer. (I was the one who had the job to say that the fast was complete.) The night that we were first intimate after the fast, there were many tears and questions that allowed for further healing. I think it gave my husband insight about the depth of my wounds.

—Jessica

In preparation for writing this book, I conducted intensive interviews with nearly thirty women whose husbands were addicted to pornography. In addition, I have heard the stories of countless women over the years after they've heard my testimony at women's retreats and conferences. If I have learned anything, it's this: of all the issues related to this contemptible addiction, none is as controversial, personal, and potentially damaging as the issue of sexual intimacy with your husband after betrayal.

Can we just talk? You know, girlfriend to girlfriend? I have heard some things over the years that have made me sick to my stomach, spitting mad, and heartbroken at the same time. I give you my word, you will *not* hear me tell you that you have a biblical responsibility to have sexual intercourse with your husband once a week (or more) to ensure that he won't be tempted by pornography. Neither will you hear me affirm that it's a good thing that you haven't been sexually intimate with your husband in the last three years.

Before I continue, I feel a responsibility to remind you of something I said in the introduction to this book. *If your husband has had an affair, paid for prostitutes, or raped you or someone else, what you are about to read may or may not pertain to you.* This book is meant to help you deal with your own issues and feelings regarding your husband's addiction to lust, masturbation, and pornography. Naturally, this will have ramifications for the marriage bed; however, criminal behavior introduces additional issues I'm not prepared to address here.

I believe you are reading this book because it's your heart's desire to walk in victory.

What would it look like to walk in victory in the area of sexual intimacy with your husband?

I have listed several thoughts other women have shared about intimacy. Mark the ones that have been your thoughts.

- I feel like I'm being used.
- I'm afraid I'm being compared to pictures of other women.
- I think having sex will only contribute to the problem.

- It's difficult to be intimate with someone who makes you furious.
- I don't think he's really "there" when we're being intimate. His mind is elsewhere.
- I wonder if every "new idea" came from an outside source.
- I don't think I can be intimate with someone I can't even talk to.

Every one of those thoughts is legitimate. Legitimate, but not necessarily accurate. I think we have to be careful here, because (if you are like me) sometimes our thoughts get in the way of our heart's cry. We can think ourselves right out of doing something that's good for us.

Likewise, your thoughts can convince you to do something you are not really ready to do. You may think you must submit to sexual intimacy with your husband because it is biblically commanded. You don't want to make him angry, or you believe it might lessen his desire to look at pornography. Perhaps you believe it's the only way the two of you can feel like you're one.

None of these is the reason you should be saying yes, nor will they produce the kind of intimacy God intended you to enjoy in your marriage. Sexual intimacy is part of his design, and we need to look at that design in the context of intimacy after betrayal. After all, marriage and intimacy are God's doing. When you are ready to say yes to sexual intimacy with your husband, it should be because you already have emotional and spiritual intimacy. You should be able to say yes and mean it with all of your heart.

Genesis 2:24 says, "Therefore a man shall leave his father and his mother and hold fast to his wife, and they shall become one flesh." Do you know who said this? The author of Genesis. Jesus indicated that that writer was Moses (Luke 24:44), and Moses was inspired by God. Therefore, what Moses wrote were God's words. In Matthew 19:4–5, Jesus said, "Have you not read that he who created them from the beginning [*God*] made them male and female, and said [*Who said? God said!*], 'Therefore a man shall leave his father and his mother and hold fast to his wife, and they shall become one flesh'?" (italics mine).

It's important to grasp the weight of this. Genesis 2:24 is the Word of God. Those words and the meaning behind them were his doing, including the part about "becom[ing] one flesh." Becoming "one flesh" certainly includes sexual union, but we mustn't forget that it also includes becoming one spiritually and emotionally. It's a coming together of two spirits or souls, and bodies. While marriage is intended for companionship and pleasure, more importantly it exists to glorify God. This is more obvious when we see Genesis 2:24 quoted in Ephesians 5:31–33.

In your Bible, read Ephesians 5:31–33. What does verse 32 tell us that marriage echoes?

Marriage is intended to echo the union of Christ and his "bride," the church. I want you to hold this truth close to your heart. You see, until you and your husband can enjoy spiritual intimacy, you can't enjoy sexual intimacy as God designed it. The first step in healing sexual intimacy in your marriage is to work toward emotional and spiritual healing.

God has plenty to say about adultery and its ramifications.

Read Proverbs 5:15–23:

Drink water from your own cistern, flowing water from your own well.
Should your springs be scattered abroad, streams of water in the streets?

Let them be for yourself alone, and not for strangers with you.

Let your fountain be blessed, and rejoice in the wife of your
youth, a lovely deer, a graceful doe.

Let her breasts fill you at all times with delight; be intoxicated
always in her love.

Why should you be intoxicated, my son, with a forbidden
woman and embrace the bosom of an adulteress?

For a man's ways are before the eyes of the LORD, and he
ponders all his paths.

The iniquities of the wicked ensnare him, and he is held fast in
the cords of his sin.

He dies for lack of discipline, and because of his great folly he is
led astray.

As we examine this passage, I offer a warning. Sexual sin is a
slippery slope. While you chose to read this book because of your
husband's addiction, do not presume that you are safe from a fall
yourself. Feelings of rejection and betrayal have landed more than
one Christian woman in the arms of a man other than her husband.
Be careful about pointing fingers as you read God's Word here. The
caution in this passage is no less true for women.

You are like water that God has put in your husband's personal
well. Likewise, your husband is the water in your well. God intends
us to draw from our own cistern for spiritual, emotional, and sexual
intimacy. Sharing the degree of intimacy God intended for marriage
with someone other than your spouse is like dumping your stream
of water in the dirty streets.

Read Jeremiah 2:13:

"My people have committed two evils:
they have forsaken me, the fountain of living waters,
and hewed out cisterns for themselves, broken cisterns that can
hold no water."

Name the broken cisterns you and your husband have dug. Why can't they hold water? I'll get you started.

Hers	His
Romance novels—set up for disappointment	Masturbation—not intimacy as God intended

Choosing pornography as a means of sexual fulfillment is one broken cistern your husband dug. As a result, you have felt poured out. God, the fountain spring, provides the abundant life. Whenever we seek other sources of fulfillment (including pornography), we are digging our own cisterns and declaring our independence from God. His plan to fill your cistern with the water he has chosen is perfect. Apart from him, we only have ourselves to draw upon.

When your husband's addiction first comes to light, it is reasonable—even *encouraged*—that you and he take a sexual fast. By that I mean that you are not sexual for a period of time—days, weeks, or months, but not years. This includes self-gratification. Of course self-gratification would also be wrong for you—not just for this season, but anytime. This does not mean that you cannot hug or kiss your husband. Sometimes you just need to be held.

I desperately needed to be wanted, needed, and loved. Even the first night he told me, after our huge fight and me telling him to leave . . . he was going to sleep on the couch, but I couldn't bear it. I screamed and cried and pushed him away, but in the end he was the only one there to hold me, so I let him.

—Lisa

If we were sitting together at the foot of your bed with a box of tissues between us, this is what I would tell you. (Remember, we're working under the assumption that your husband's addiction stayed at Level I or II, which is the focus of this book.) Assuming that you and your husband both desire to work toward restoring every facet of your marriage, you first need to renew your friendship with him. Start acting the way you would like to feel about your husband, even if you don't yet feel that way. In other words, be kind, considerate, and fun. Do things together that you both enjoy. Watch a movie, go on a hike, tackle yard work, or complete a project. Whatever you do, create a team feeling. The goal here is to remember that you still really like this guy and enjoy being with him. This is how you probably established emotional intimacy before you were married. It can work again.

Then you need to talk to each other about the important things, especially your feelings regarding sex. It is exceptionally difficult to demonstrate vulnerability during intercourse if you feel angry, afraid, embarrassed, or hurt. Am I right? You have to talk to your husband about these feelings. It's essential that when you stand naked in front of your husband, you feel emotionally cared for and safe. Sharing your concerns about intimacy with each other, and accepting and respecting what you hear, will go a long way toward healing.

As your emotional intimacy is strengthened, you need to begin touching each other in nonsexual ways again. Perhaps this hasn't been an issue for you and your husband, but many couples don't get within arm's length of each other after the pornography addiction is made known. This is the time to hold hands, hug, kiss, and snuggle in bed with no expectations. You don't have to do all of these, and perhaps there are other physical touches that you prefer. It's your responsibility to make them known to your husband and his to make his requests known to you. Now is the time to share what you like as well as where you draw the line. See what you can do to honor each other by respecting and satisfying these requests.

Read 1 Corinthians 7:5: "Do not deprive one another, except perhaps by agreement for a limited time, that you may devote yourselves to prayer; but then come together again, so that Satan may not tempt you because of your lack of self-control."

What does this passage say you are to be doing during this period of abstinence? Why do you think this is critical?

To everything there is a season. There's a season to fast and a time to break the fast. When the time is right, and you have reconnected emotionally and spiritually, then it's time to make a move toward reconnecting sexually. I don't want you to get into a pattern of withholding intimacy from your husband.

God does not avert his eyes when a husband and wife are sexually intimate. Neither should you take your eyes off him when you are intimate with your husband. We cannot separate out the spiritual aspect of sexual intimacy. The physical desire (not to be confused with a need) that a husband and wife have for each other is God-given. We honor him when we are able to fully share ourselves again with our husbands.

It takes time. On the one hand, I want you to be patient, gentle, and kind to yourself. You have experienced a deep wound, which will take time to heal. On the other hand, do not be tempted to use the gift God has given you as a means of wreaking vengeance on your husband. Doing this will only clear a path for Satan to continue the damage to your marriage he began with the pornography.

I'm going to offer a few ideas for you and your husband to consider implementing when you are ready to be sexually intimate. Encourage your husband to verbally ask you if you'd like to be sexual with him. This will help you feel respected and will allow you the freedom to say no with honesty and without repercussion. If you are concerned that your husband's mind drifts to old images when the two of you are intimate, leave the lights on or candles lit. This way you can see each other's eyes. When he's truly seeing you, you'll be assured that he is fully present. Finally, pray together before you are intimate and ask God to be part of this. Prayer alone can transform the act of sex from feeling bad, evil, ugly, and secret to the beautiful gift God intended it to be.

Journal Assignment:

I know firsthand how hard it is to discuss sexual intimacy. Many of us have gotten the impression in church that this is not something that good Christian women discuss. Silence is the enemy of sexual healing in your marriage. If you anticipate that it will be difficult to discuss what you need with your husband, start by writing it in your journal. Maybe you have never allowed yourself to ask for what you need and desire in this area. Here is your chance. Remember, sexual intimacy is God's doing. He isn't frowning at you right now. He desires your pleasure.

Day 5: Needs, Desires, Longings, and Yearnings

I need him to start by being totally honest with himself and me. I need him to act like a husband and care about my needs and concerns, to hear me and to be here for me physically, emotionally, spiritually, financially, and sexually.

—Sarah

Needs. Desires. Longings. Yearnings. In an effort to choose my words carefully, I've discovered that a fine line separates the meaning behind each of these words. Here is my quandary: needs are necessities, required for survival, if you will. Labeling something a need should not be taken lightly, in my opinion. I confess that my needs are often easily confused with my wants. Then there are desires. These are things I long or hope for. If I'm not careful, my *desires* can morph into thinly veiled de*mands,* which is not very attractive. I am drawn to the term *longing,* but by its very definition, it suggests that what is strongly desired is unattainable. Well, how unsatisfying is that?

So here I am at *yearning,* which means a tender or urgent longing—and because there is no mention in the definition of it being unattainable, I'm willing to settle here. The significance of choosing the most precise word is not to be missed. You see, we all have yearnings, which distinguish the contours of our heart. They clarify what makes us the unique women we are, and they give shape to our purpose for living life abundantly. Sometimes our yearnings are tender and quiet, and other times they scream with urgency to be fulfilled.

In the midst of my husband's addiction to pornography, my yearnings felt more like longings—strong desires that were seemingly unattainable. As I went through long seasons of unmet longings, their original clarity began to blur until I couldn't have told you what I needed, what I desired, what I longed for . . . I couldn't have told you what I yearned for.

In the midst of your mess, have you lost sight of your deepest yearnings? We can find assurance in the fact that through the long, dark nights there is One who knows.

> O Lord, all my longing is before you;
> my sighing is not hidden from you.
> (Psalm 38:9)

Read John 21:1–14 in your Bible.

Whose voice did the disciples hear after their long, empty night?

What do you suppose possessed the disciples to follow through with Jesus' unconventional request?

What did Jesus have waiting for them when they made it to shore?

Don't miss this, because after long, dark, empty nights, when your soul aches because of unmet longings, if you listen, there is One who is asking you to trust him. He is intimately aware of your longings and he is so crazy in love with you that his desire is to meet your needs, even if it's just breakfast on the beach. He wants you to be filled.

Did you notice anything funny about verse 11? Read it again.

It says there were 153 fish in the net. 153. Let that sink in a minute. Someone. Counted. The. Fish.

They pulled in the net, which was bursting with fish, and were awestruck that it didn't tear in two. When you pull in your heart, you may discover that even while it feels broken, it hasn't torn in two. In fact, there are more blessings in your net than you dreamed possible. When you take a moment to count them, you recognize that they didn't get there from any effort on your part. Without asking who did this, you recognize the Lord's fingerprints all over it. "And from his fullness we have all received, grace upon grace" (John 1:16).

It would be so easy to focus on the "have nots" here. We could list and lament all our unmet yearnings—our longings. Or we could count our fish.

Name some of the ways the Lord has shown you grace upon grace.

The Lord spoke to my heart the night my husband told me of his addiction. He told me to "Hang on and do your part. I will use your story for MY glory." I clung to those words like they were my last breath of air. At times, I would repeat them over and over. I think God knew I needed something tangible to cling to in the dark of night and in the lonely moments.

—Jessica

I have books piled on my desk as I write this, each of which describes what various authors believe are the desires of a woman's heart. As I've read each author's ideas, I have found myself creating my own categories. Some agreed with several authors, others not so much. I believe there are three yearnings that most, if not all, women share. They are:

- To know and be known
- To be someone's beloved
- To be nurtured

I don't doubt that as you read my descriptions of each of these, you may enthusiastically agree with some of them while you reject others and create some categories of your own. I'm not offended. I don't pretend to have the inside scoop on the contours of your heart. I want you to begin to define your personal yearnings in light of your current circumstances, as well as *in spite of* your current circumstances.

Most of us long *to know and be known*. One of our deepest desires as wives is to know our husbands. When he shares his thoughts, feelings, and yearnings, we feel as though he's letting us into his life. Likewise, when there is a long stretch of silence, we assume he's cutting us out. Knowing our husband brings us to a place of trust where secrets can't hide. We are confident that there isn't a gap between the person *we* know him to be and who he actually is.

When we authentically know our husbands, it invites us to allow ourselves to be known. We are able to strip away the public veneer and share our own secrets, wounds, and yearnings, knowing that they will be heard and understood without condemnation. We are accepted and loved for who we are, just as we are.

Most women desperately want *to be someone's beloved—* someone's one and only, loved unconditionally. As someone's beloved, you become his partner, playing an irreplaceable role in accomplishing God's purpose for you as a couple. You are confident that you are an essential part of the union. Wouldn't you agree that when your husband chooses to make you his top priority, right after his relationship with Christ, you feel loved and fulfilled?

As someone's beloved, you are unquestionably beautiful and desirable in his eyes. In the deep recesses of your heart, do you long to be desired? In *Captivating*, John and Stasi Eldredge wrote, "Every woman has a beauty to unveil. Every woman. Because she bears the image of God. She doesn't have to conjure it, go get it from a salon, have plastic surgery or breast implants. No, beauty is an *essence* that is given to every woman at her creation."[1] In response to that beauty, we yearn to be desired and chosen. The bottom line is that you desire to be desired by the one who calls you beloved—your husband.

Do these yearnings reflect your heart? Before we go on, take a moment and make some notes.

How do these yearnings fit in the context of your current circumstances?

To know and be known . . .

To be someone's beloved . . .

Finally, we yearn *to be nurtured*. Check out the definition for *nurture*.

> **nur·ture** *v*: 1. To give tender care and protection to a young child, animal, or plant, helping it to grow and develop. 2. To encourage somebody or something to grow, develop, thrive, and be successful. 3. To keep a feeling in the mind for a long time, allowing it to grow or deepen.[2]

To be nurtured is to be on the receiving end of tender care, protection, and encouragement. Is your heart safe in your husband's care? As women, we extend our hearts to the one our soul loves. We trust him to protect it with everything he has. We long to be comforted and to receive mercy. We want nothing more than to place our physical, emotional, spiritual, financial, and sexual well-being in the hands of our husbands and experience an incredible sense of security. This is a place where we can grow, take chances, and experience an intimate connection with the one God chose for us.

In a nurturing relationship, we are deemed worthy. As a result, we are able to walk in confidence, assured that we have been justly evaluated and found to be lovable and valuable—as is. We need not fear failure because we know that the one who finds us worthy will be on life's journey with us, encouraging, supporting, celebrating, and grieving alongside us. A husband's affirmation of our worth has the power to fill us with hope for the future.

Nurturing also includes touch. Michelangelo once said that "to touch can be to give life."[3] I think he was onto something. In an article entitled "Hands On Research: The Science of Touch," Dacher Keltner cites the research of neuroscientist Edmund Rolls and concludes that "touch signals safety and trust, it soothes. Basic warm touch calms cardiovascular stress. It activates the body's vagus nerve, which is intimately involved with our compassionate response. A simple touch can trigger release of oxytocin, aka 'the love hormone.' "[4] I don't think it takes a neuroscientist (though it doesn't hurt) to tell us that God wired us to connect with others by touch. I'm talking about safe, tender, nonsexual touch—a back rub, holding hands, or a passing caress of the arm. We need it from the day we're born until the day we go home to be with the Lord.

To be nurtured is to feel at home in your own skin, as well as in the arms of the man you love.

How does the yearning to be nurtured fit in the context of your current circumstances?

Read Proverbs 13:12 and 19a: "Hope deferred makes the heart sick, but a desire fulfilled is a tree of life. . . . A desire fulfilled is sweet to the soul . . . ."

In light of your longings (those desires that have seemed unattainable), what does Proverbs 13:12 and 19a say to you?

Read Psalm 37:4: "Delight yourself in the LORD, and he will give you the desires of your heart." This is probably fairly familiar. Unfortunately, we often don't hear it paired with the verse that follows: "Commit your way to the LORD, trust in him and he will act" (v. 5).

We can't skip over the parts about delighting, committing, and trusting and still expect God to give us our desires. I know what you're thinking. I have asked myself the same question at different seasons: "If God gives me the desires of my heart, why is my husband still addicted to pornography?"

Read these verses in context in Psalm 37:3–7a:

> Trust in the LORD, and do good; dwell in the land and befriend
>   faithfulness.
> Delight yourself in the LORD, and he will give you the desires of
>   your heart.
> Commit your way to the LORD; trust in him, and he will act.
> He will bring forth your righteousness as the light, and your
>   justice as the noonday.
> Be still before the LORD and wait patiently for him; fret not
>   yourself over the one who prospers in his way, over the man
>   who carries out evil devices!

Don't despair; this psalm holds instruction and a promise for you. You are not meant to put your delight in your husband but in your relationship with Jesus Christ, your Lord. That must be first and foremost. Then you must "trust in the LORD and do good." This is no time for self-sufficiency and vengeance.

The Scripture also says you must "commit your way to the LORD [and] trust in him." Let me make this simple. Is it going to be your way or Yahweh's? Choose. (How is your way working out so far anyway? This choice is really no choice at all, is it?)

Day 5: Needs, Desires, Longings, and Yearnings

Last but not least, you are commanded to "be still before the LORD and wait patiently for him." Ouch! The "w" word and the "p" word in the same sentence. Seriously? Yes. You need to wait and keep waiting until he chooses to give you the desires of his heart, in his timing. There it is—the crux of the matter. Is your desire in line with God's desire for you? Ask him to align your heart with his.

> I think God can meet our needs so much more intimately and deeply than we think. It's often, however, not in the *way* we think we need . . . or in the time line that we often think we require. And I know there were probably times when I sabotaged "receiving" *him* and his gifts to me because I was too self-focused.
>
> —Evelyn

You can't begin to fathom the yearnings your Father has for you, yet his greatest desire is to be desired *by* you. He is constantly looking into your heart to see if you long for him. Ask him to give you the desire to yearn for him more than anything else, because he alone can fulfill all of your heart's yearnings.

> I will give them a heart to know that I am the LORD,
> and they shall be my people and I will be their God,
> for they shall return to me with their whole heart.
> (Jeremiah 24:7)

We've spent the last five chapters soaking in truths about trust—what it looks like and how to restore it—in the midst of a husband's addiction to pornography. Be patient. Wait. Trust will either be built or destroyed in the countless choices you and your husband make minute by minute, day by day, week by week, year by year. I encourage you to place your wounded heart in the hands of the One who knows the pain you have experienced and the yearnings that both whisper and scream in the depths of your soul.

131

Yes, God is able to meet my needs when I dial into him as my Source rather than into my husband. The ability to allow God to meet my greatest needs is a long learning process. It is a dance done over years, not weeks or months . . . and almost always has been learned best when I am broken.

—Olivia

Journal Assignment:

I have been talking to God about you today, and I have been reminded that he wants you to know that he loves you and you can trust him. "The LORD your God is in your midst, a mighty one who will save; he will rejoice over you with gladness; he will quiet you by his love; he will exult over you with loud singing" (Zephaniah 3:17). Take his hand and let him pull you into his embrace. He is able to keep pace with you, sweeping you into a holy dance with him. In your journal, whisper your heart's yearnings into his attentive ear . . . and don't forget to thank him for the fish.

IDENTITY

WEEK 4

Day 1: Pursued and Chosen

I simply wanted my husband to choose me over "them"—the images he lusted after. I wanted to be enough.

—Nicole

i·den·ti·ty *n*: essential self: the set of characteristics that somebody recognizes as belonging uniquely to himself or herself and constituting his or her individual personality for life.[1]

The color of your hair and eyes, your height and weight, education, career, and personal accomplishments might identify you on your driver's license and professional resume, but they don't really tell anyone who you are, what makes you tick, or how you perceive yourself. Who you believe yourself to be shapes the way you present yourself to others, the way you treat them, and the way you permit them to treat you. What you think about your identity also determines how much joy you experience in life. Most important, it affects the way you interact with God.

Much of your identity is built on the foundation of what you believe about the following things: whether you were chosen, God's design for your life, how you measure up to others, your self-worth, and your ability to be irreplaceable.

I have looked into the faces of many women whose husbands are addicted to porn (for that matter, I have looked in the mirror). I recognize the eyes of a woman for whom each of those building blocks of identity has been shattered. Do you have those eyes? I imagine you collected the broken pieces and began to rebuild your identity, but the damaged pieces didn't fit the way they did before the devastation. *I wasn't chosen. What's wrong with me that God would allow this to happen? If only I was as beautiful as she. I thought I alone could meet his needs, but apparently I'm replaceable.* When you stepped back to look at the self you attempted to reconstruct, you didn't recognize this new identity. Whose face is reflected in your bedroom mirror now?

I must confess that when I married, I made my husband the foundation of my identity. This was all my own doing; I'm not pointing fingers at him. My entire identity was defined by my relationship to my husband, and when the cracks in that foundation were discovered, my identity came crumbling down. Family and friends who had known me my entire life will tell you that at that time, I was a shell of my former self. For the most part, my exterior looked the same, but nearly every aspect of my personhood, those things that defined my identity before and after that season, was absent. It was a case of missing identity.

In the next five chapters we are going to tiptoe through the broken pieces of your identity. Then we are going to place those pieces in the hands of the Almighty Creator because he alone has intimate knowledge of your value. He knows exactly who he made you to be.

Chosen

My chiropractor recently told me about a radio show he often listens to called *War of the Roses*. Before I tell you the gist of the program, let me assure you that I did my homework, and though the show exists, it is done completely with paid actors. In other words, it's fake! Nonetheless, the premise is that a woman in a committed relationship believes she is being cheated on and contacts the radio show. The radio personality calls the allegedly unfaithful partner and, with the initiator listening silently on the phone line, creates a ruse to get the "cheater" talking. Often the suspect is told that he has won a dozen roses to be delivered to anyone he chooses. (You can see where this is going, can't you?) This is about the time the allegedly unfaithful one either outs himself or makes the silent woman on the phone—who is praying, *Pick me! Choose me!*—very happy.

Even as a radio reality show, it's a sick game to play, in my opinion. I can't find pleasure in eavesdropping on the breaking of a woman's heart.

We long to be chosen. Most of us have childhood memories of waiting with our classmates, our backs to the wall, while two peers stand in front of the group and alternately choose their teams. "Pick me!" Countless opportunities to be chosen present themselves in the ensuing years, until we find ourselves on college graduation day looking toward our future. "Choose me!"

Then we pray that the man God has chosen for us will pursue us until he finds us—the perfect fit—and chooses us for his life partner. A wife feels and becomes beautiful when she is confident that she is loved. Being pursued and chosen tells us something about ourselves—or so we believe. We seem to think it sounds like this: *Pursued. Chosen. Loved. Beautiful.*

When the sin of pornography is discovered, the truth that porn was chosen over you cuts to the quick. Now a new chant pounds in your ears: *Rejected. Inadequate. Unloved. Undesirable.* Few things are as painful as rejection. I know.

I have a question for you, and I don't want a head answer; I want a heart answer. In other words, please don't tell me what you know to be true and what you think the right answer is. Tell me how you feel on your hardest days—straight from the heart.

Since learning about your husband's addiction, how has your sense of who you are (the core of your identity) changed?

Many women whose husbands are seeking healing in their personal lives and in their marriages have told me that their husbands have assured them that their decision to turn to porn had *nothing* to do with their wives. I believe it. There are books filled with the reasons why men get lured by pornography. Among the best of those books is *Healing the Wounds of Sexual Addiction* by Dr. Mark Laaser. In it he says, "It is in the deep and fertile ground of chaos, dysfunction, silence, and abuse that the seeds of sexual addiction are sown."[2] Examining family-of-origin issues will be critical to your husband's healing.

But remember, you aren't here to fix your husband. I am sharing this information to help you understand that his decision to choose pornography was not a conscious decision to reject you. Your feelings and the truth are often not the same things. You *feel* rejected, inadequate, and undesirable. The *truth* is that the pornography is not about you. (I know that your husband might have told you something to the contrary in the midst of his addiction, but it's not true. God says so. Whose word are you going to believe?)

Read John 1:12: "But to all who did receive him, who believed in his name, he gave the right to become children of God."

What does it mean to you to know that God loves you so much that he calls you his child?

In your Bible, read Ephesians 1:4–11.

Did you catch that? It says that "he chose [you] in him before the foundation of the world, that [you] should be holy and blameless before him" (v. 4). Your being chosen was "predestined according to the purpose of him who works all things according to the counsel of his will" (v. 11). As I type these words, I am praying with all my strength that you will cling to the realization that *God chose you.*

What does it mean to you that your *Abba* Father specifically chose *you*?

I hope you understand that even though God has already chosen you and called you his child, he continues to pursue a relationship with you. He longs to be with you. He is totally sold out for you. You were worth the price his Son paid for you on the cross. Even as you pursue a deeper relationship with him, your Bridegroom chases after you.

> Set me as a seal upon your heart, as a seal upon your arm,
> for love is strong as death, jealousy is fierce as the grave.
> Its flashes are flashes of fire, the very flame of the LORD.
> Many waters cannot quench love, neither can floods drown it.
> If a man offered for love all the wealth of his house, he would
>   be utterly despised.
> (Song of Solomon 8:6–7)

When you pick up the damaged piece of your identity that cries, "My husband didn't choose me," remember that the One who knows you best chose you and pursues you still. For a time, you may have allowed yourself to be wrapped in a cape of lies that makes you feel rejected, inadequate, unloved, and undesirable. With each truth you are about to hear, I pray that you will unfasten that dark cape that hangs like a noose around your neck. Toss it aside and allow God to envelop you in his cloak of grace. He knows you intimately; nothing escapes his notice.

> Where shall I go from your Spirit? Or where shall I flee from
>   your presence?
> If I ascend to heaven, you are there! If I make my bed in Sheol,
>   you are there!
> If I take the wings of the morning and dwell in the uttermost
>   parts of the sea,
> even there your hand shall lead me, and your right hand shall
>   hold me.
> If I say, "Surely the darkness shall cover me, and the light about
>   me be night,"
> even the darkness is not dark to you;
> the night is bright as the day, for darkness is as light with you.
> (Psalm 139:7–12)

You can put on your I've-got-it-all-together face for the rest of the world, but God sees right through it.

Match the following passages to the truth it reveals about how God sees you.

In his Word he writes:

For he will command his angels concerning you to guard you in all your ways. On their hands they will bear you up, lest you strike your foot against a stone. (Psalm 91:11–12)

Because God sees me as:

Competent

You were ransomed from the futile ways inherited from your forefathers, not with perishable things such as silver or gold, but with the precious blood of Christ, like that of a lamb without blemish or spot. (1 Peter 1:18–19)	Chosen
Not that we are sufficient in ourselves to claim anything as coming from us, but our sufficiency is from God, who has made us competent to be ministers of a new covenant. (2 Corinthians 3:5–6)	Valuable
For we are his workmanship, created in Christ Jesus for good works, which God prepared beforehand, that we should walk in them. (Ephesians 2:10)	Lovable

Rejection always hurts, but when it comes from your husband, the wound is particularly deep. I'm not minimizing that in the least. You long to be chosen and still pursued by your life mate. There is nothing you can do to make that happen yourself. However, Jesus knows what rejection feels like. He is the only One who can turn your husband's heart toward him and toward you, so pray. Pray specifically so that when God answers, you will have no doubt that it was his hand at work.

Most importantly, remember that while there is nothing you can do to make your husband pursue and choose you, there is nothing you *need* to do to make God pursue you, except to be still and let him catch you. He is the One you want and need because only he can fill the empty spaces in your heart. He yearns for a lifelong relationship with you. He says, "Daughter, my heart aches for you, and I will search for you until I find you. You are mine. I love you to pieces. You are more than adequate—you are perfect. I made you that way in Christ. I choose you."

Day 2: God's Design

I had a discussion with God, and he told me that my life was like a book. I was reading along, and all of a sudden, I came to a chapter that I did not want in my book. I wanted to tear those pages out, but since I was not the author, I couldn't do that. And he reminded me that he was going to use our story for his glory and that he was the author. He reminded me that what Satan intended for evil, he would use for good. He would write my story, and this chapter needed to be in there for the ending to come out right. I wanted desperately to change the storyline or discard those pages altogether, but what God has written as a result of that chapter has been wonderful. He has redeemed what the locusts have eaten. He has restored the years that were lost. He didn't just rebuild the torn-down castle, he replaced it from the foundation up. It is brand new. And it is good.

—Melissa

We have a nasty habit of internalizing faulty beliefs about who God designed us to be and what he intended to become of our lives. If we didn't already have issues before porn pulled its steamer trunk full of filth, pain, and conflict into our marriages, then we most certainly did afterward. *Doesn't God want me to be happy? Have I done something that would cause him to do this to me?* No and no. We'll unpack the reasons why in this chapter.

I recently spoke at a one-day conference entitled "I Have Learned to Be Content." I was the keynote speaker, and I taught on Philippians 4:11–13 (NIV).

Read the first two verses for yourself.

> I am not saying this because I am in need,
> for I have learned to be content whatever the circumstances.
> I know what it is to be in need, and I know what it is to
>   have plenty.
> I have learned the secret of being content in any and every
>   situation,
> whether well fed or hungry, whether living in plenty or in want.

I was fairly confident that I knew what it meant to be content until I studied the Greek text of Philippians 4:11. I discovered that the Greek word *autarkes* (ow-tar'-kace), which we translate as *content,* really has nothing to do with our emotional state of satisfaction. Rather, *autarkes* means "self-sufficient, self-reliant, or self-complacent."

Now, don't get upset. Paul wrote these words, and we know he wasn't like the first-century Stoics who taught that human happiness can be gained with a DIY (do-it-yourself) mind-set. He isn't suggesting, "For I have learned to be *self-sufficient* whatever the circumstances." No, throughout Philippians, Paul clearly teaches the centrality of Christ for living according to God's design. Let's see if we can figure out what he's saying.

Reread Philippians 4:11–12. What two things did Paul "learn"?

1.

2.

Paul says he had to *learn* to be content and he *learned* the secret of being content, which implies that there was a time in his life when he didn't know how to be content. (That makes me feel better, because I know I haven't attained perfect contentment; I'm still learning.) If you don't know how much it cost Paul to learn this lesson, take a moment to read 2 Corinthians 11:24–28. You won't find pornography on that list, but I wouldn't trade places with Paul for most of the things he experienced. Yet he learned contentment. Paul was an old, gray-haired man when he wrote these words. It took him a lifetime of lessons to learn to be content.

Stick with me as we move in on our target. Paul says in Philippians 4:12, "I have learned the secret of being content in any and every situation" (NIV). FYI, Paul is not a very good secret keeper.

Paul spills the beans in the next verse. Read Philippians 4:13 and write it here.

Take note: Paul isn't about self-sufficiency at all. He is about Christ-sufficiency. He is wholly relying on Christ as his source of strength. Happiness is temporary and based on our circumstances, but contentment is independent of our circumstances and based on the degree to which we rely on Christ. It's as though Paul is saying, "I have learned the secret of being *Christ-dependent* in any and every situation." Don't miss this. You, too, must be Christ-dependent in every situation, including your present circumstances. God has little concern for how happy you are, because he hasn't promised you happiness. He is, on the other hand, most interested in how content, holy, and "his" you are. Your contentment is found in your relationship with Christ.

> Count it all joy, my brothers, when you meet trials of
>   various kinds,
> for you know that the testing of your faith produces steadfastness.

And let steadfastness have its full effect, that you may be perfect
and complete, lacking in nothing.
(James 1:2–4)

Ephesians is a great book to read when you are trying to locate
your missing identity and grasp God's design for your life. The
first two chapters of this epistle tell you who you are as a new creation in Christ Jesus. There is great tension between the "already"
and the "not yet." That is, everything we are about to read in
God's Word is *already* true of you, even if you have *not yet* experienced it fully. This is all about who you are, not what you do; and
it's independent of who your husband is or what choices he makes.
Trust me on this. God said he sees you this way. You'd better
believe it.

Read Ephesians 1:1–14 in your Bible. Then list the ways God
already sees you.

I am _____ (1:3)

I am _____ (1:4)

I am _____ (1:5)

I am _____ and _____ (1:7)

I am _____ (same as v. 4) (1:11)

I am _____ (1:13)

God wants you to know how he sees you in Christ. You are
blessed, chosen, predestined, redeemed and forgiven, and sealed in
Christ Jesus with the Holy Spirit. You are his masterpiece.

. . . having the eyes of your hearts enlightened,
that you may know what is the hope to which he has called you,
what are the riches of his glorious inheritance in the saints . . . .
(Ephesians 1:18)

For we are God's masterpiece.
He has created us anew in Christ Jesus,
  so we can do the good things he planned for us long ago.
(Ephesians 2:10 NLT)

The Greek word translated "masterpiece" is *poiéma* (poy'-ah'-mah), which is also the word "poem." You are God's poem. Every line of a poem, with its unique cadence and emphasis, is essential for understanding and appreciating subsequent lines. Likewise, in your life story, every previous chapter has left its mark on the chapter for today, and today's chapter will shape the chapters to come.

What does it mean to you that God says you are:

An original masterpiece.

Created anew.

Intended to do good things.

Meant to act according to his plan.

I wonder if you might have clenched your teeth or sensed a catch in your spirit when you filled in the blank next to what it means to you that God says you are "meant to act according to his plan."

I had that kind of reaction. Whose big idea was your husband's addiction to pornography anyway? God's? Did he cause your husband to sin? Was this all somehow part of his great plan for you? Absolutely not. God will not now, nor will he ever, cause a man to sin. Choosing to engage in the sin of pornography was a product of your husband's will. There are numerous passages that demonstrate that God intends for—no, commands—us to exercise our will to make righteous decisions. (These passages include Deuteronomy 30:15–16; John 14:15; 1 Corinthians 9:24; and 1 Timothy 6:12. Don't take my word for it; look them up!) God did not include pornography—and the fallout that results—in his design for your marriage, but he is so incredibly efficient that he will use it all to redeem the pain you have experienced.

> . . . The LORD has anointed me to bring good news to the poor,
>> he has sent me to bind up the brokenhearted,
> to proclaim liberty to the captives,
>> and the opening of the prison to those who are bound;
> to proclaim the year of the LORD's favor,
>> and the day of vengeance of our God;
>> to comfort all who mourn;
> to grant to those who mourn in Zion—
>> to give them a beautiful headdress instead of ashes,
> the oil of gladness instead of mourning,
>> the garment of praise instead of a faint spirit;
> that they may be called oaks of righteousness,
>> the planting of the LORD, that he may be glorified.
> They shall build up the ancient ruins;
>> they shall raise up the former devastations;
> they shall repair the ruined cities,
>> the devastations of many generations . . . .
> Instead of your shame there shall be a double portion;
>> instead of dishonor they shall rejoice in their lot;
> therefore in their land they shall possess a double portion;
>> they shall have everlasting joy.

For I the LORD love justice;
>I hate robbery and wrong;

[*Note: I'm sure he hates pornography too.*]

I will faithfully give them their recompense,
>and I will make an everlasting covenant with them.

Their offspring shall be known among the nations,
>and their descendants in the midst of the peoples;

all who see them shall acknowledge them,
>that they are an offspring the LORD has blessed.

I will greatly rejoice in the LORD; my soul shall exult in my God.
(Isaiah 61:1b–4, 7–10a)

I did not choose pornography. (I'm sure you didn't either.) God did not choose it for me either. However, when my husband chose pornography, God inserted a parenthetical moment into the story of my life. In the space between those parentheses, he assured me that I wasn't alone. He knew my pain. He saw my tears. He felt my losses and he would redeem it all. He did.

Today, because of the relationship I have with my Bridegroom, I count it a privilege to have had my life interrupted by that sacred set of parentheses. I firmly believe that the covenant of marriage may ultimately be more about a woman's relationship with God than her relationship with her husband.

Do you agree that the covenant of marriage—by God's design— might be more about your relationship with God than about your relationship with your husband? If so, how does that change your attitudes and expectations?

Does God want me to be happy? No, he wants you be content, holy, and his. Will he give you joy? Most certainly, but it will be delivered out of a relationship with him that has nothing to do with your past, present, or future circumstances.

Have I done something that would cause him to do this to me? No, God did not cause your husband to sin, and though your husband's choice ushered in an army of repercussions, God can and will "restore to you the years that the swarming locust has eaten . . . . You shall . . . praise the name of the LORD your God, who has dealt wondrously with you. And *my people* shall never again be put to shame" (Joel 2:25–26, italics mine).

Journal Assignment:

> "If you abide in me, and my words abide in you,
> ask whatever you wish, and it will be done for you."
> (John 15:7)

Take a few minutes to sit quietly at the Father's feet. Ask him to reveal to you his perfect design for your relationship with him. Ask him to show you the person he sees you to be. (Listen carefully, using Scripture, so that you are sure to hear his voice and not the old, familiar voice of the deceiver.) Write the answers in your journal. Tell God you would like to exchange the ashes from the pornography inferno for his beauty.

Day 3: Comparison Trap

I had horrible body image issues before I met my husband. He was my first boyfriend and the first guy to tell me he loved me for me. While I think part of me always loathed my body, it felt wonderful to have someone find me beautiful. After I found out about my husband's sexual sin, my body image issues compounded hugely. I knew in my head that I wasn't the problem and that even if I were a supermodel my husband could struggle with this issue, but wrapping my heart around it was difficult and some days impossible.

—Amelia

I have a tendency to use my looks as a way to gain attention and affirmation from my husband and other men in hopes of having my emotional needs met. I find myself to be very critical of other women, and I compare myself to them in an attempt to make myself feel more acceptable.

—Stephanie

I'm going to be honest with you. Most mornings I look in the mirror and think, *How did* that *happen?* If I weren't already discontent enough with myself, I hear hundreds of media messages every day telling me that I have very good reason to be discontent. I flip on the morning news shows, and in no time at all I'm certain my skin isn't quite as smooth as it should be, I'm way too fluffy, and my teeth could stand to be whiter. My bladder, my digestive system, my hair, my makeup, my food intake, my exercise routine—none of them are up to snuff according to the media. Advertisements promise: "Use me, buy me, eat me, drink me, wear me, put me in your hair" and you will be 'beautiful.' "

Did you know that every year Americans spend an average of $12.4 billion on cosmetic surgery[1] in a futile attempt to attain physical perfection? If women banded together and agreed to look in the mirror and say to their reflection, "Darling, you look gorgeous!" I believe the multibillion-dollar cosmetic industry would go belly-up. (Don't get me started on bellies. Please!)

What is beauty anyway? Sometimes my teenage daughter and I completely disagree about what's beautiful and what isn't. She has informed me that just because I'm the mom, my definition of beauty doesn't automatically trump hers. Oh, really? Then who gets the last say on beauty? Hollywood? Modeling agencies? Fashion magazines? Do we get to vote?

I don't know who determines the cultural standards for beauty, but I do know that the more I hear about beauty and see it promoted on TV and in magazines, the more I find myself believing that what "they" say must be right. Then I peek in the mirror again and . . . sigh . . . .

I don't know a single woman who hasn't sipped from the dangerous cocktail of pride, vanity, consumerism, and unhealthy comparisons. Add a husband's pornography addiction to the mix, and the tendency to compare oneself to others goes up exponentially.

The women I've talked to with a husband who uses porn have stumbled upon or searched until they found evidence of the addiction. Is that your story too? Are the images you saw on the screen or on magazine pages seared into your memory? Are the "other women" right there in your head? Do you see them when you close your eyes at night? Me too.

May I take a moment to draw your attention to something? *If your husband is talking with you about his addiction, how does he refer to it? Does he use the same words you do?* Porn. Lust. Addiction. Or does he refer to it as "it"? "'It' started when . . ." "I'm struggling with 'it' today . . ." "'It' isn't a problem anymore." In a physical affair you would be hearing about "she," and in your heart you may be feeling like it certainly is a "she" who was chosen over you. Am I right? But your husband probably would never refer to his addiction as "she" because for him there is no individuality about the women he ogles. They all belong to a collection—"it." It is much harder to compare ourselves to a thing called "it" than to an airbrushed "her," isn't it?

> If I could share some wisdom with other women who are just now going through an ordeal similar to mine, I would want to tell them that they are beautiful, and even if they were super-models and had perfect behavior, it probably would have still happened.
>
> —Lynne

Oh, if only we could power-wash the images off our cerebral cortex and remember them no more! We need to lay those memories down. Take a minute and pray with me right now.

> Lord, hear my prayer. Listen to my cry for mercy; in your faithfulness and righteousness come to my relief. You say in your Word to forget the former things and not to dwell on the past because you are doing a new thing. Please help me to forget, Father. Replace the pictures in my head with a new portrait of true beauty that you have for me. Amen.

Describe what the new portrait of true beauty might look like.

The reality is that when we are feeling rejected and our self-esteem is in the toilet, it may be tempting to try to compete with the porn models. Please don't do it. Can you say "digitally enhanced"? Porn is a multibillion-dollar industry, and believe me, those girls' images are airbrushed and "photoxed" to artificial perfection. (Yes, I made that word up.) All you need to do is sneak a peek at tabloid covers featuring the un-enhanced faces of makeup-free celebrities. They look—gasp!—shockingly not much different than you or me (blemishes and all). Then you will realize that the women in *Playboy* or on Internet porn probably don't look gorgeous without digital enhancement either. Suddenly our imperfections seem less significant, wouldn't you agree?

Our God has plenty to say about beauty. In fact, his Word seems to confirm the fact that there are two types of beauty—authentic and phony (my words, not his). Let's see if you can define each type yourself before we come to the end of this chapter.

Read each of the following verses. Underline the words that best exemplify God's definition of authentic beauty *or* expose phony beauty. Circle the word that describes which type of beauty is being described.

Who is like the wise? And who knows the interpretation of a thing? A man's wisdom makes his face shine, and the hardness of his face is changed. (Ecclesiastes 8:1)
Authentic or *Phony*

Day 3: Comparison Trap

The LORD said: Because the daughters of Zion are haughty and walk with outstretched necks, glancing wantonly with their eyes, mincing along as they go, tinkling with their feet, therefore the Lord will strike with a scab the heads of the daughters of Zion, and the LORD will lay bare their secret parts. (Isaiah 3:16–17)
Authentic or *Phony*

Put on then, as God's chosen ones, holy and beloved, compassionate hearts, kindness, humility, meekness, and patience. (Colossians 3:12)
Authentic or *Phony*

And behold, the woman meets him, dressed as a prostitute, wily of heart. She is loud and wayward; her feet do not stay at home . . . . (Proverbs 7:10–11)
Authentic or *Phony*

I desire then . . . also that women should adorn themselves in respectable apparel, with modesty and self-control, not with braided hair and gold or pearls or costly attire, but with what is proper for women who profess godliness—with good works. (1 Timothy 2:8–10)
Authentic or *Phony*

But let your adorning be the hidden person of the heart with the imperishable beauty of a gentle and quiet spirit, which in God's sight is very precious. For this is how the holy women who hoped in God used to adorn themselves . . . . (1 Peter 3:4–5)
Authentic or *Phony*

Did you discover that sometimes the description of phony beauty told us as much or more about authentic beauty? As Scripture showed us what not to wear and what not to do, we were learning lessons about what we *should* wear and do. Do you think you can define authentic beauty and phony beauty yet? Let's try.

Based on God's Word, see how many elements of the two types of beauty you are able to list.

Authentic Beauty   Phony Beauty

Did you come to the realization that authentic beauty is about an eternal, inward, spiritual beauty within your heart and soul, while phony beauty is about external, physical beauty that can often be purchased in a bottle, off a rack, or at a doctor's office in the form of makeup, diet pills, vitamins, food, clothes, and plastic surgery? Hollywood evaluates beauty based on physical appearance. The pornography industry evaluates it based on physical appearance and sexual performance. God utilizes an entirely different paradigm, and guess what? He gets the final word on the matter.

> Charm is deceitful, and beauty is vain,
> but a woman who fears the LORD is to be praised.
> (Proverbs 31:30)

God doesn't make junk. Yet I know that on some deep, seemingly untouchable level, there may be a part of you that believes the deceiver's lies that parts of you are too ugly to be loved. You know the truth about what God thinks of you and how he sees you, yet you find yourself using the woman across the room, on TV, or in *People* magazine as your measuring stick. You fall into the comparison trap.

I sometimes sense the Holy Spirit telling me to skip the flowery words and tell it like it is. This is one of those times. Buckle up for some brutal honesty.

(1) You *should* care how you look. Your body is a temple, and you have a holy responsibility to be in good health and to care about your physical appearance. If subconsciously you are sabotaging your physical appearance because you don't want your husband to be drawn to you, then you need to wrestle that one to the ground. Stop it. And if you can't stop it, get yourself some counseling. I'm serious.

(2) You should want to look and feel your best, *but* God is very concerned about whether you are in bondage to superficial means of altering your appearance. Search your heart, and honestly assess if you have gone too far.

(3) Jesus wants you to quit comparing yourself to others and to start comparing yourself to him. Look in the mirror. Who do you see? If he deems it necessary, God will do some serious spiritual nipping and tucking until you look more like him.

(4) You were made in the image and likeness of your Creator (Genesis 1:26). Good luck finding anything more beautiful! He formed you before your mama even knew you existed (Psalm 139:13). You are unique; there is no one like you in existence because you were fearfully and wonderfully made (Psalm 139:14). He had a purpose in mind for you when you were born (Ephesians 2:10). Though you are broken, you are loved, redeemed, and called (Romans 3:9–12, 23; Romans 8:38–39; Hebrews 10:14; 2 Timothy 1:9). You are his and that is a fact you cannot change. Your identity is in him, and nothing and no one can change that.

Journal Assignment:

The comparison trap is easy to fall into because looking at others to see how we measure up, rather than looking at Jesus to see who we are, is an old, nasty habit. In your journal, write about the different "measuring sticks" you have used to evaluate yourself, and see if you measure up.

When you are tempted to go near that old trap again, claim God's Word. Write Proverbs 29:25 in your journal using either the ESV or *The Message*. Then recite it thirty times. Yes, that's *thirty* times. It won't take long, and when you're done, it will be hidden in your heart—and there when you need it.

> The fear of man lays a snare,
> but whoever trusts in the LORD is kept safe.
> (Proverbs 29:25 ESV)

> The fear of human opinion disables;
> trusting in God protects you from that.
> (Proverbs 29:25 *The Message*)

Put a tick mark on each of the thirty blanks below as you recite it.

_ _ _ _ _   _ _ _ _ _   _ _ _ _ _   _ _ _ _ _   _ _ _ _ _   _ _ _ _ _

Day 4: Self-Worth

> Because I know who I am in Christ, my self-worth has remained
> intact. What I don't understand is why my husband, whom God
> has called to love me, can't seem to recognize that worth and
> value. That's what hurts. I feel abandoned, betrayed, sold out.
>
> —Sarah

Praise God that Sarah, in the vignette above, came out with a rela-
tively unscathed sense of self-worth because she understood and
accepted her identity in Christ. While her husband's lack of understanding hurts her, it hasn't shaped her.

Sadly, most women I talk to believe that their husband's choices
reflect the truth about their own value. They believe "If his choices
seem to indicate that he thinks I'm worthless, I must be worthless."
That is a lie from the pit of hell.

Three perceptions influence our sense of self-worth: how others
perceive us, how we perceive ourselves, and how God perceives us.
Spoiler alert! Rather than waiting until the end of the chapter to
summarize the lessons we're about to uncover, I'm going to give
you the bottom line now and tell you that only God's perception
counts.

Unfortunately, a woman's self-concept or sense of her own value often tends to be based on what others in her sphere of influence do and say. Old messages from childhood, as well as messages from her husband, continually play in her mind. In this chapter, I want to give you a way to reprogram those thoughts and discover your true value according to what God *did* for you and who he *says* you are in Christ. It's all about actions and words. We can allow them to determine our negative self-worth *or* shape a healthy, biblical sense of self-worth.

Read Psalm 8:3–5:

> When I look at your heavens, the work of your fingers,
> the moon and the stars, which you have set in place,
> what is man that you are mindful of him,
> and the son of man that you care for him?
> Yet you have made him a little lower than the heavenly beings
> and crowned him with glory and honor.

Underline the last line in this passage.

How is your sense of self-worth shaped by the fact that the Creator made you a little lower than the heavenly beings and crowned you with glory and honor?

I think there is a danger in thinking too little of ourselves *or* too much of ourselves. In either case we can get preoccupied with thinking too much *about* ourselves—period. This can taxi us to the brink of unhealthy comparisons again, leading to self-righteousness (which we will tackle in Week 5, Day 1) or self-deprecation.

Regardless of where your self-perception barometer stands right now, I want you to know that you can walk in victory in this area. Let's take a look at two biblical examples of men with low self-perceptions and the outcome of their way of thinking.

Read the following verses. After the first passages, record the words that describe the men's self-perception. After the second passage, record the outcome.

Initial Condition	Final Outcome
Job	
Job 9:21 and 23:1–12	Job 42:10–17

Caleb and Joshua after exploring Canaan	
Numbers 13:30 and 14:6–9	Numbers 14:28–35

**The other men who
explored Canaan**

Numbers 13:31–33   Numbers 14:28–35
(focus on v. 33)

Did you notice that even when Job lacked a keen awareness of
God's activity in his life—a life he despised—he knew that God
saw him? He chose to stay close to God and believe his words (Job
23:11–12). *Proximity to the Author of life first changed Job's heart
and then changed his circumstances.*

I hope you also noticed the difference between Caleb and Joshua
and their fellow explorers or spies. Caleb and Joshua did not catch
the "Grasshopper Syndrome" that their partners did. This syndrome was characterized by a severe case of low confidence in God
and his promises, which resulted in even lower self-confidence.
(Note: Self-confidence often registers at the same level as self-worth
on our self-perception barometer.)

Caleb and Joshua were confident in God's word and his ability
to act according to his word. I think these two would have fully
embraced Paul's New Testament declaration that "I can do all
things through him who strengthens me" (Philippians 4:13).

Never forget that *what you think often determines what you
believe is going to happen and thus dramatically influences how
you will act and/or what you will say.* In this case, what Caleb,
Joshua, and their comrades thought determined what they believed
would happen if they entered Canaan. This radically influenced
what they said to Moses. Caleb and Joshua stuck to their faith-guns,
and God moved them—and them alone—into the Promised Land
forty years later. Their comrades (brought low by the Grasshopper
Syndrome) died in the wilderness of a severe case of unbelief and

disobedience. As the Bible puts it, they "died by plague before the LORD" (Numbers 14:37).

We give many things the authority to determine our self-worth: lack of education, tragedies and abuse from our past, body image, and sin, to name a few. Each has the ability to define our current sense of value if we allow it.

Address each of the things that tend to suck the self-worth out of you.

	What have others said?	What do you think?
Do the academic degrees (or lack of degrees) hanging on your wall determine your value as a person?		
Do the evil intentions of someone from your past warrant self-reproach today?		
Has emotional/physical/sexual abuse at the hands of a loved one (parent, sibling, husband, extended family member), friend, or stranger deprived you of worth in all circumstances since?		
Do the numbers on the bathroom scale determine your ability to love or be loved?		
Has personal sin given you a case of the Grasshopper Syndrome?		

My heart is racing because I wish I could know what you think. Have you bought into the lies? Do you know the truth? Remember what I told you earlier: *What you think often determines what you believe is going to happen and thus dramatically influences how you will act and/or what you will say.*

What does Proverbs 28:26 tell us that should serve as a caution?

Read Jeremiah 17:9. What does it say about the heart?

I have tears running down my cheeks and onto the keyboard as I write this. Please *do not* miss this! If you allow the actions and words of anyone but Christ to define the way you think, it will take root in your heart, which is why we are given strict instructions in Proverbs 4:23.

In bold letters, write Proverbs 4:23.

Underline it. Highlight it. Do whatever it takes to remember the source of your negative self-evaluation, because what takes root in your heart will influence how you will act and what you will say from here on out. Confronting the roots of your negative self-image is essential for your spiritual healing in the midst of your husband's addiction to pornography. Dealing biblically with these issues will determine whether you will be able to contribute to healing in your marriage.

In the end, what others have said or done and what you have thought, said, or done must not be permitted to define your worth. Your worth is revealed in the gospel. It is where we see what the Father *did* for you through his Son and who he *says* you are in Christ. It's very likely that you have to change the way you have been thinking, isn't it?

God gives us his Word to help us reprogram our thinking. Before

I give you your assignment, you must promise to actually *do* it. Just reading the model won't result in changed thinking.

Reprogramming your thinking will take three steps. Each will take time. Don't rush it.

Step 1: Using an exhaustive concordance or an online tool (I highly recommend www.biblegateway.com—"match exact phrase"—for this assignment), search for all the New Testament verses that reveal what God says about your identity in his Son. Search for the following phrases and mark them in your Bible:

- In Christ
- In him
- In the beloved
- In whom
- Through Christ
- Because of Christ
- With Christ

Step 2: In your journal, rewrite these verses as a positive declaration of who you are. For instance, paraphrase Romans 8:1: "There is therefore now no condemnation for those who are in Christ Jesus." You could write, "I am not condemned because I am in Christ Jesus."

Step 3: To replace your old, negative thoughts with new ones, you must repeatedly think the new thoughts. Remember, "Whatever is true, whatever is honorable, whatever is just, whatever is pure, whatever is lovely, whatever is commendable, if there is any excellence, if there is anything worthy of praise, think about these things" (Philippians 4:8). I am asking you to commit fifteen minutes a day, for as long as it takes, to the essential work of replacing the lies you've clung to about your self-worth with truth from God's Word.

- Find a place and time where and when you can be uninterrupted. Get comfortable. Relax.
- Think about the last time you were with someone else and you engaged in negative self-talk. You told yourself you are worthless, incapable, unattractive, and deserved the

situation in which you found yourself. Remember what you
said to yourself. How did you express it to the other person?
What did you say or do? Play it back, scene by scene.

- Now turn it off. Replay it again, but this time tell yourself
the truths you listed in your journal. Be convincing. Say it
like you mean it.
- Envision yourself doing and saying things that reflect the
truth about who God says you are, what he says you can
do, and what you have through his Son.
- Stop and listen to the Holy Spirit bringing truth and
affirmation to your heart. "Well done, daughter. Well
done."

But you are a chosen race . . . a people for his own possession,
that you may proclaim the excellencies of him
who called you out of darkness into his marvelous light.
(1 Peter 2:9)

I'm so proud of you! I believe that when you begin thinking
about yourself in the same terms that Christ thinks of you, and as
you believe your worth is determined by your Savior, you will begin
acting and speaking in a way that reflects and restores your God-
given dignity. I pray that when you brush off the residue of your
husband's addiction, embrace your self-worth in light of who you
are in Christ, and reflect this truth in your actions and speech, your
husband will have no choice but to agree with your value. However
(and this is big, so listen carefully), while changing your thinking
about your value *might* influence your husband's thinking, that is
not your motive for change. Your motive is to glorify your Father
by accepting and respecting what *he* says about you.

Remember, how your husband or anyone else perceives you is
inconsequential in defining your actual worth. How you see yourself in light of how God sees you is all that matters.

And from where he's sitting, you're looking good!

Day 5: Irreplaceable

Sometimes I would wake up at two in the morning and realize he hadn't come to bed . . . again. I'd sneak down the hallway and see the glow from the computer peeking out from under the closed office door. Sometimes I'd knock on the door or throw it open, but most times I tiptoed back to my empty bed and cried into my pillow, then feigned sleep when he'd slink in and try to slip into our bed without waking me. I was sexually available and willing, but he never initiated intimacy, and when I tried to, he always had a lame reason why he couldn't. He'd obviously found a more pleasurable option for having his sexual needs met than with me.

—Nicole

union *n*: the act of joining together people or things to form a whole.[1]

By its very definition, the word *union* implies that without it, the people or things are not whole, but partial or incomplete. I think that's why God created man and woman and said, "Therefore a man shall leave his father and his mother and hold fast to his wife, and they shall become one flesh" (Genesis 2:24). This is why we watch chick flicks. When the complications in the lives of the main characters are finally untangled, and they profess their undying love because "together we are complete," we heave a sigh of satisfaction. I believe this is why little girls and young women dream in fairy tales.

> Once upon a time there was a beautiful princess who married a dashing prince. He had great riches, but he loved her more than wealth. A hundred friendships surrounded him, but he loved her more than friends. When he was exhausted and feeling sorry for himself, he loved her more than comfort and ease. When temptations pranced before him and lust whispered his name, he kept their marriage bed pure and loved his beautiful princess more than sex. The prince loved his wife more than his own life. The only thing he loved more was his father the King. And because of that, they lived happily ever after.

Sigh . . .

Most women desire to meet the needs of their husbands that are uniquely theirs to meet. Those needs include the emotional and the relational, but more critically, the physical needs. We long to be irreplaceable in all these areas.

From the moment you discovered your husband's sexual betrayal, no doubt you felt the sting of being replaced by numerous digitally enhanced women who never get tired after caring for children all day, who are always available and ready, who never retain water or have bad hair days, and who always say the right things. You became replaceable to your husband, at least in terms of his physical needs, and it broke your heart.

Were you told by in-laws, well-meaning friends, pastors, and counselors to "be more of a woman" or to "go home and fulfill (your husband's) sexual needs" to make everything better? This only damages and confuses your identity. First, it communicates that you are insufficient and thus worthless. Second, it suggests that you are in a position to fix your husband, which you are not.

The definition of lust is "the strong physical desire to have sex with somebody, usually without associated feelings of love or affection."[2] Your husband has an addiction to lust, which he attempts to satisfy with pornography. However, rather than satisfying lust, porn feeds it. Porn addicts, consequently, are on a quest to satisfy their insatiable desires. Part of the "turn on" is that the activity is forbidden and dangerous. Lest you have forgotten, let me remind you that your marriage, by definition, is anything but "forbidden and dangerous." This is why nothing you can do will satisfy that addiction.

There is, however, a Bridegroom who deems you irreplaceable. Brennan Manning describes this union, this oneness with Christ.

No human word is even remotely adequate to convey the mysterious and furious longing of Jesus for you and me to live in His smile and hang on His words. But *union* comes close, very close; it is a word pregnant with a reality that surpasses understanding, the only reality worth yearning for with love and patience, the only reality before which we should stay very quiet.[3]

Read the following passages from Song of Solomon:

"My beloved is mine, and I am his" (2:16).

"I am my beloved's, and his desire is for me" (7:10).

What do these passages tell you about the Bridegroom's commitment to you?

Your relationship with Christ is exclusive. There is no room for anyone to intrude in this intimate relationship. As one who has been sanctified by the shed blood of Christ, union with him is what you should seek. It's the essence of belonging. You are his, and he is yours.

I could tell you that God loves you because he made you (Ephesians 2:10). Without question he loves you because you desperately need him. (You and I are pretty pathetic without him.) I might be able to make a pretty strong case for his loving you because he realizes your potential (Isaiah 64:8 and 2 Timothy 2:20). I'm fairly certain he loves you because you are valuable to him. You cost him his Son, after all.

But I don't believe any of those are the real reason he loves you. I believe he loves you because he *chooses* to love you.

> But God, being rich in mercy, because of the great love with which he loved us, even when we were dead in our trespasses, made us alive together with Christ—by grace you have been saved—and raised us up with him and seated us with him in the heavenly places in Christ Jesus. (Ephesians 2:4–6)

You can hear an echo of this kind of love in this quote from *The Alchemist,* by Paulo Coelho.

> "I'm going away," he said. "And I want you to know that I'm coming back. I love you because . . . ."
> "Don't say anything," Fatima interrupted. "One is loved because one is loved. No reason is needed for loving."[4]

What does it mean to you to hear that God loves you just because he chooses to do so?

Day 5: Irreplaceable

Why do you love in general? In particular, why did you first love your husband?

Did you first love your husband because of the way he made you feel? The way he looked at you? Was it his goofy wit, his intelligence, or perhaps his unshakable integrity? What if that changed? Then what happens to your love? (Don't answer that. Just consider it.)

Why did your husband first love you?

This question packs a whole lot of potential trouble, doesn't it? Was it your figure? Your free spirit? Your availability? And might that have changed over time?

This is thin ice we're skating on because every possible response to why you first loved your husband or why he first loved you implies a conditional love. What if any one of those reasons for loving changes? Then what?

"[You are your] beloved's, and his desire is for [you]" (Song of Solomon 7:10 NASB). God doesn't love you *because* of who you are, what you look like, how you act, or what you say, but *in spite of* who you are, what you look like, how you act, and what you say.

Record Malachi 3:6a here.

God's love is not determined by anything about your unique but ever-changing character. He loves you because he chooses to love you in the context of his immutability. He does not change. Could we ever really trust the Word of God if his character was always changing? How could we ever rely on that? We couldn't. But his character traits are woven throughout Scripture without contradiction. Remember, "Jesus Christ is the same yesterday and today and forever" (Hebrews 13:8) and "every good gift and every perfect gift is from above, coming down from the Father of lights with whom there is no variation or shadow due to change" (James 1:17). In other words, God loves you, and that will never change—even when you do. There is absolutely nothing you can do about it.

I remember clearly the dark night of my soul when I lived far from family and no one knew the excruciating secret I kept for my husband. One night I drove my car to the parking lot of a country church, miles from the city lights. I locked the doors, turned off the engine, and pulled a box of tissues close. Feeling very alone, I sought out my Savior and proceeded to place every broken fragment of my heart into his capable hands. *Abba Father, I am yours. I need someone to hold me. I hurt so badly. I'm not my husband's one and only. He doesn't need me. He doesn't want me. I've been replaced.*

After a while, I started my car and prepared to leave, but before I put the car into gear, I rested my forehead on the steering wheel, stealing another moment to collect myself. That's when a song began to play through my car speakers.[5] The words washed over my broken heart as an a cappella group sang Christ's song to me. He reminded me that I wasn't alone, that he knew my pain and sorrowed with me. He assured me that no matter what my deceived heart might tell me, he saw me as perfect and blameless. As the music filled my car, I rested in the truth that I didn't deserve this and that he would make the wrongs right.

I can't begin to tell you how that song ministered to my soul. Nor am I going to tell you how many times I listened to it in that parking lot before I finally drove away. My heart had found its way home.

I was his and no one (not even a computer-enhanced image) could ever be like me. I was irreplaceable. Hallelujah!

> Up! Escape to Zion, you who dwell with the daughter
>   of Babylon.
> For thus said the LORD of hosts, after his glory sent me
>   to the nations who plundered you, for he who touches you
>   touches *the apple of his eye.*
> Behold, I will shake my hand over them, and they shall
>   become plunder for those who served them.
> Then you will know that the LORD of hosts has sent me.
> (Zechariah 2:7–9, italics mine)

You are the apple of God's eye. Scripture doesn't just tell us this once, but four times. In addition to the passage you just read, Deuteronomy 32:10, Psalm 17:8, and Proverbs 7:2 all refer to the apple of his eye and describe it as something to be protected. You can trust and believe that he knows the fragility of your heart right now. There is nothing that escapes God's attention. If it touches you, it touches his eye.

When you fully embrace the truth that Christ's desire is for you, nothing will ever be the same. You will delight in the truth that he has chosen you and that he will pursue you until the day he brings you home. He is in the business of restoration. He is going to restore the years the locusts have eaten and redeem the pain you have experienced. You will look in the mirror and see how much you reflect him, rather than comparing yourself to others to determine your worth.

You will read Zephaniah 3:17–18, 20 . . .

> "The LORD your God is in your midst, a mighty one who
>   will save;
> he will rejoice over you with gladness; he will quiet you by
>   his love;

he will exult over you with loud singing.
I will gather those of you who mourn for the festival,
so that you will no longer suffer reproach. . . .
At that time I will bring you in,
at the time when I gather you together;
for I will make you renowned and praised among all the
    peoples of the earth,
when I restore your fortunes before your eyes," says the Lord.

. . . and hear him singing over you because you're his little girl. He will heal your heart because you are irreplaceable. Although the prophets originally wrote these promises to Israel, God's covenant people, believers today are part of God's new nation, chosen people and covenant family (1 Peter 2:9–10), so we hear the heart of God for us in these passages as well.

BROKENNESS

WEEK 5

Day 1: Black-and-White Thinking

I've asked a lot of you throughout the last twenty chapters. Together, we have sifted through the broken pieces of your heart and begun the messy work of putting it back together to create a new mosaic. I recognize that some of it has been painful. I hope you have felt God sustaining you, not only through our journey together in these pages, but from the beginning of this life experience.

In the next five chapters we are going to focus on Christ's specialty during his time on Earth and today—the healing of broken hearts.

> He heals the brokenhearted
> and binds up their wounds.
> (Psalm 147:3)

As you continue this journey of the broken heart, I believe you will discover that it will bring you closer to Christ's heart before it's all over. As you fix your eyes on your final destination—the arms of the Almighty—it's good to know where he can be found.

Read Isaiah 57:15 and underline the two places it says he inhabits and the people with whom he dwells.

For thus says the One who is high and lifted up,
who inhabits eternity, whose name is Holy:
"I dwell in the high and holy place,
and also with him who is of a contrite and lowly spirit,
to revive the spirit of the lowly,
and to revive the heart of the contrite."
(Isaiah 57:15)

Did you have any idea that our God chooses not only to reside in eternity in the high and holy place, but also "with him who is of a contrite and lowly spirit"? The Hebrew word translated as "contrite" is *dakka*. Found only in the Old Testament, it means "broken in spirit, cast down."[1] Sounds to me like God seeks out those who have broken hearts and takes up residence with them.

Why does he choose to dwell in this place? (Hint: reread the last line of the passage.) What does that mean for you?

Pull up a chair now and wrap your arms around that throw pillow. Can I get you anything else? I'm trying to soften the blow for what's coming next. You see, things are about to get a little uncomfortable.

If your heart is broken (and I kind of hope it is so that the Lord is residing there), then it's not *just* because you have been a casualty of your husband's porn addiction. How easy it would be to cast full blame on him. But I'm afraid you need to hear a little more information about the meaning of "contrite."

"In Holy Scripture, the heart is the seat of all feeling, whether joy or sorrow. A contrite heart is one in which natural pride and self-sufficiency have been completely humbled by the consciousness of guilt."[2]

Two words in this description cause me to catch my breath. The first is "humbled," which I'll explain in a moment. The second is the "g" word—guilt. Now there is a garment that's never comfortable to wear, as it tends to wrap itself around one's neck and squeeze. Guilt, as defined here, implies that you have a *reason* to feel guilty.

As for being humble, you realize that this is referring to *your* need to be contrite and humble, not your husband's, right? The opposite of humility is arrogance or pride, the bedfellow of self-righteousness. We will concentrate on this subject for the rest of the chapter. Why? Because when your husband is addicted to lust, porn, and self-gratification, one danger you face is seeing him as all "bad" and yourself as all "good." You may be unable or unwilling to separate his addiction from who he is apart from the deviant behavior. This requires special attention because self-righteousness is a slippery slope.

> I was really shattered by my husband's betrayal. I wondered what I had done wrong. It didn't take too long, however, for me to become self-righteous.
>
> —Dianna

Whenever you are feeling overwhelmed by your emotions, you are at high risk for black-and-white thinking. Moralistic thoughts fixate on polar opposite, either/or ideas. Your husband is either perfect or horrible, either completely right or completely wrong, either brilliant or an idiot. You might resort to black-and-white thinking any time there is an emotional crisis and flip-flop between thinking someone or something is all good or all bad. There was probably a time when you saw (or chose to see) *only* the good about your husband. Since it has been proven that your husband is addicted to pornography (bad!), you tend to put *everything* he says or does in the negative camp while you settle yourself in at Camp Sugar-and-Spice-and-All-Things-Nice.

We become especially fond of the words *always* and *never*. For instance, your husband gets home late from work one evening, which is rare. Because he was up late the night before and you suspect he might have been on the computer looking at porn (though you have no evidence), you greet him with, "You are *always* late. You *never* think about anyone except yourself!" (and a few more similar pleasantries). Really? *Always* late? *Never* thinking about anyone else? *Never*?

Let's suppose your husband was up late because he drank caffeinated coffee late in the afternoon and couldn't sleep, and he was late from work because he stopped to pick up the dry cleaning he'd heard you mention when you were on the phone with your mother. Gulp.

Because it's more comfortable to think of him as the one who's always wrong, we often have a hard time admitting when we're wrong. Sometimes, in an effort to avoid being deceived, we struggle to admit that there is a lot we don't know or understand in this situation and we must not jump to conclusions.

Describe a time when you needed to tell your husband that he was right and you were wrong regarding something involving his addiction. How did that feel? (If learning about your husband's addiction is still very fresh, you may not have an example of this yet.)

If you have engaged in black-and-white thinking, what kinds of attitudes and thoughts have you had toward your husband that may have been unfair?

Day 1: Black-and-White Thinking

Sweeping generalities escort us quickly into the trap of self-righteousness and pride.

Read 1 Peter 5:5b–6:

> Clothe yourselves, all of you, with humility toward one another,
> for "God opposes the proud but gives grace to the humble."
> Humble yourselves, therefore, under the mighty hand of God
> so that at the proper time he may exalt you.

You have a choice when you get up in the morning and look in your closet. Are you going to clothe yourself in humility toward your husband or does the jacket of pride better suit your present state of mind? I wouldn't be your friend if I didn't point out that the garment of pride makes your self-righteousness look enormous! And if you keep it on for long, you'll discover a bundle of other unflattering accessories that go along with pride.

Match the following negative effects of pride with their supporting passage. (See p. 178 for complete list.)

A. Deceives us.

_____ Live in harmony with one another. Do not be haughty, but associate with the lowly. Never be wise in your own sight. (Romans 12:16)

B. Brings destruction.

_____ Love is patient and kind; love does not envy or boast; it is not arrogant or rude. (1 Corinthians 13:4)

C. Inhibits harmony in relationships.

_____ But Hezekiah's heart was proud and he did not respond to the kindness shown him; therefore the LORD's wrath was on him and on Judah and Jerusalem. (2 Chronicles 32:25 NIV)

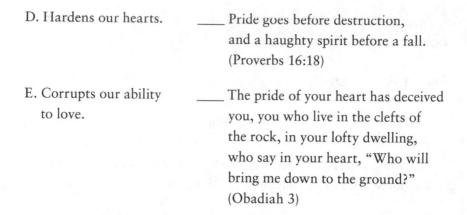

D. Hardens our hearts.　　　　_____ Pride goes before destruction, and a haughty spirit before a fall. (Proverbs 16:18)

E. Corrupts our ability to love.　　_____ The pride of your heart has deceived you, you who live in the clefts of the rock, in your lofty dwelling, who say in your heart, "Who will bring me down to the ground?" (Obadiah 3)

If you just looked in the mirror and realized that you are wearing that old black-and-white jacket of pride again (in fact, it looks rather worn since it's become a favorite), then I suggest that you spend some time with the Lord until you find a garment of humility to wear. "God opposes the proud but gives grace to the humble. Submit yourselves therefore to God" (James 4:6–7), and trust him to tell you what not to wear.

Please don't misunderstand what I'm saying here. I am not suggesting in any way that you put on blinders and walk in denial about truly bad behavior on your husband's part. Setting boundaries and refusing to listen to lies is not self-righteousness. However, continuously serving as judge and jury of your husband and finding him guilty for *everything*, including sharing the air you breathe, may tip the scales toward self-righteousness.

Black-and-white thinking can be a fruitless attempt to fill an empty spot left by poor self-worth. When you feel bad because of the choices your husband has made, a part of your brain says you are better than he is and certainly more deserving. The degree to which you try to feel better about yourself by making your husband feel worse will correspond to the degree to which you fail to allow God to take care of that hole in your heart. "In the pride of his face the wicked does not seek him; all his thoughts are, 'There is no God'" (Psalm 10:4).

178

Day 1: Black-and-White Thinking

When you have a broken heart, it may feel like everything else hurts too, and it's hard to change clothes when you hurt everywhere. I have a few suggestions that will gently lead you away from the black-and-white section of your closet.

(1) Add shades of gray to your wardrobe. Don't classify every action and word spoken by your husband into two categories. It might not feel comfortable at first, but extend grace to him. Realize that his behavior and words can be both good and bad, right and wrong, and sometimes may fall right in the middle of the two.

(2) Surrender control of your life and situation to God so that one day you might say, "I have fought the good fight, I have finished the race, I have kept the faith. Henceforth there is laid up for me the *crown of righteousness,* which the Lord, the righteous judge, will award to me on that Day, and not only to me but also to all who have loved his appearing" (2 Timothy 4:7–8, italics mine).

(3) Recognize that you may look good most of the time, but you are not *perfect.* You are no more always right and good than your husband is always wrong and bad. To be honest, sometimes you're a mess. Welcome to life as a woman walking with God. I promise that if you draw near to him, you will begin to look more and more like him, but it is a process, not an event. As of yet, you are unfinished (see 1 John 1:10).

(4) God didn't flub up on you or your husband. Remember that the next time you are tempted to see everything as black or white. Each of you is created in the image of God, though each of you has a sinful nature that has damaged that image by sin. (Note: Pride that masquerades as humility wails, "I'm pitiful, worse than, homelier than, worthless," but it is still pride.)

Read James 4:11–12:

> Do not speak evil against one another, brothers.
> The one who speaks against a brother or judges his brother,
> speaks evil against the law and judges the law.
> But if you judge the law, you are not a doer of the law,
> but a judge. There is only one lawgiver and judge,
> he who is able to save and to destroy.
> But who are you to judge your neighbor?

When you surrender your tendency to judge to the One who is able to save and destroy, you will be free from the trap of pride and self-righteousness. You will cast off the garments of black-and-white thinking, and you will never desire to put them on again.

Journal Assignment:

List specific ways you intend to be mindful about avoiding black-and-white thinking, especially when it comes to your husband, but in other situations as well. Set some goals for yourself. Remember—take baby steps. For instance, this week, each day I will find one example of "shades of gray" rather than make sweeping generalities about my husband.

Day 2: Looking in the Magnified Mirror

God has taught me that sin is sin. I have sinful aspects of my nature that appear less harmful, but isn't all sin harmful? It's what separates us from the love and intimacy God can give us. I've realized that the number one sin, or the original sin of man, is self-centeredness. When we think of gratifying our own needs and look inward more than outward, the sins fester and break open and ooze out of our being. Some aren't as recognizable because they become "the norm"—we see this sin in our everyday life (for example, the sin of overspending). All we have to do is look out the windows of our homes and work to see the self-indulgence. What we fail to see is the view others see when they look in our windows.

—Stephanie

A broken heart is not necessarily a reflection of brokenness. Consider that for a moment.

When you describe yourself as "brokenhearted," you are attempting to describe your heart's condition—how you feel. Brokenness, however, isn't the result of something that's been done to you. It is a choice you make to surrender your will to God's will in your life.

What's more, this isn't an event, but a process of daily letting go of self-righteousness and totally depending on God.

Brokenness is a good thing. Are you surprised to hear me say that? It's true. When you allow God to pulverize the hard parts of your heart, you can receive his truth. The truth is then able to take root in the soft soil of your heart, where it will grow. You probably remember from the last chapter that the definition of *contrite* is "broken in spirit, cast down." It can also mean "crushed, literally powdered."

Most days I convince myself that I have successfully disguised my hard clods of self-reliance by accessorizing with my Bible and squirting a few spiritual-sounding words behind my ears and on my wrists. I peek in the mirror and ask, "Mirror, mirror, on the wall, who's the most self-righteous of us all?" Then I hurry away, lest I hear the answer I fear: "You. That's who!"

I'm afraid that sometimes it's necessary to look in a magnified mirror. I say this with a bit of trepidation because, well, have you ever looked at your face in a 10x magnified mirror? No one needs to see her face that close. Seriously! However, most of us need to look at our hearts that closely now and then to identify those hardened places that need to be offered to the Lord for breaking and softening.

I suspect that you have developed some hard places in your heart since you've learned about your husband's addiction. It may not have happened overnight, but you need to look at those hard places—and fast. For healing to occur, you must admit and become accountable for your own shortcomings. (I hope you noticed how quickly I attempted to say that last line so it wouldn't hurt so much—sort of like ripping off a bandage.)

Describe your initial reaction to the suggestion of using a magnified mirror to identify your own sin issues.

Day 2: Looking in the Magnified Mirror

Are you thinking, *Why should I have to address my issues? He's the one with the addiction! I didn't do anything wrong!* Listen to Eugene Peterson's interpretation of Matthew 7:1–5 in *The Message*.

> Don't pick on people, jump on their failures, criticize their faults—unless, of course, you want the same treatment. That critical spirit has a way of boomeranging. It's easy to see a smudge on your neighbor's face and be oblivious to the ugly sneer on your own. Do you have the nerve to say, "Let me wash your face for you," when your own face is distorted by contempt? It's this whole traveling road-show mentality all over again, playing a holier-than-thou part instead of just living your part. Wipe that ugly sneer off your own face, and you might be fit to offer a washcloth to your neighbor.

I'm not asking you to take inventory of your own character issues and sin because I somehow believe your husband's addiction is your fault. It isn't. I've told you that before, but I don't want you to forget it.

The purpose of this book, remember, is to take you on a journey to discover how your broken heart can become a work of splendor in the masterful hands of God. That can't happen if sin is keeping you from the Designer. "Behold, the LORD's hand is not shortened, that it cannot save, or his ear dull, that it cannot hear; but your iniquities have made a separation between you and your God and your sins have hidden his face from you" (Isaiah 59:1–2).

Maybe it *feels like* the pie chart illustrating the sin in your marriage would show that your husband's piece consumes 98 percent of the pie and yours only covers 2 percent. But God doesn't compare one person's guilt to another's. His standard is himself and his holiness, not your husband's sinfulness. This is your chance to take 100 percent of your guilt and surrender it to the Almighty so that he can deal with it. It may not feel good. That is as it should be. A growth zone is never a comfort zone, and a comfort zone is never a growth zone. Even as God takes up the hardened clods of your sin and refines them, he will teach you lessons about humility, compassion, and surrendering.

I had always had my own demons of insecurity. At twelve, I lost my dad, and within a month of his death, my friends in the sixth grade all signed a note saying they didn't want to be my friends anymore . . . . It wasn't any fun. Since I had been a part of the "popular" group, I had no friends. The ironic thing is that I became a Christian the summer after my dad died, but the scars had already formed. These scars have followed me into adulthood and have made me very untrusting of friends. I have a great fear of abandonment. I tend to push people away before they can push me away.

—Nora

I have been right where you're sitting. I remember thinking, I'm *not the one who stayed up night after night looking at smut. I didn't take any clandestine trips. I didn't have a secret post office box or run up phone bills to feed my perversion. What do I have to confess?* I can tell you now that I had plenty to confess. But on the days when my husband wanted me and everyone else to believe our marital problems were *all* my fault and he was the innocent party, I wasn't willing to admit any of those sins! I was sure that admitting my shortcomings would validate his accusations.

Take a deep breath. Exhale.

I had to learn that admitting my sins and taking responsibility for them was between God and me. Even when I was still spitting nails and cut to the core because of my husband's betrayal, I couldn't blame him for the barrier I was creating between me and my Savior.

Possible Areas of Sin

"If we say we have no sin, we deceive ourselves, and the truth is not in us" (1 John 1:8).

Circle all that apply to you. My thoughts and/or actions have been characterized by/as:

- Adultery
- Anger
- Anxiety/worry
- Arrogant
- Bitterness
- Boastful
- Careless with body
- Carousing
- Complaining
- Compulsive
- Condoning
- Critical spirit
- Deceit
- Discord/fighting
- Disrespectful
- Dissension
- Don't pay debts
- Drunkenness
- Envious
- Exaggeration
- Faithless
- Fear
- Fits of rage
- Frustration
- Gluttonous
- Gossip
- Greedy
- Hatred
- Heartless
- Hypocrisy
- Idolatry
- Impatient
- Inadequacy
- Indifferent
- Inferiority
- Lacking self-control
- Lustful fantasies
- Malicious
- Murderous thoughts
- Nagging
- No fruit of the Spirit
- Not compassionate
- Not gracious
- Not merciful
- Not praying
- Obsessive
- Procrastination
- Refusing to submit
- Ruthless
- Sarcastic
- Self-indulgent
- Sexually immoral
- Slandering my husband
- Superiority
- Tell coarse jokes
- Tempted to stray
- Unfaithful
- Unforgiving
- Ungrateful
- Unkind
- Use obscenities
- Waste time
- Withholding intimacy

I do not believe all sins are equal. Some sins are further down a spiral of depravity, which result in more damage to the soul of the sinner and greater consequences for others. These sins are worse in the sense that they make it harder to turn back to God, and the collateral damages are far worse. However, please listen to me carefully here: Every single sin on that list will separate you from God. Just because Level 4 sexual sin is worse than telling coarse jokes on the downward spiral of depravity, that doesn't exempt the jokester from separation from God, nor does it mean that Jesus would not need to atone for it. Every sin on that list comes straight out of Scripture where the authors address virtues and vices. All of us have vices, and none are acceptable. Each one separates us from the Love of our life. This is why we must daily repent before God.

I feel the Holy Spirit urging me (beyond a gentle nudging) to specifically address one sin some women are prone to when their husbands are addicted to pornography. That is their own fall into infidelity. When a man is investing his energies in pornography, he often has less interest in his wife's ability or desire to meet his sexual needs. As a result, a woman who is seeking affirmation, affection, and intimacy may be tempted to look outside the marriage for emotional or sexual fulfillment. It is essential that a woman ask others to hold her accountable in this area. She must avoid isolating herself. Do you remember the natural progression from our thoughts to our beliefs to our actions? The same progression happens with infidelity. The sin of adultery often begins in your thought life, with daydreams and fantasies. The next thing you know, you are talking about it or beginning an emotional affair with someone. Before you know it, you have sinned in deed.

It's also essential to explore any deep wounds you received long before you knew about your husband's struggle with pornography. In fact, these wounds may have existed before you even knew your husband. Perhaps you dealt with them some time ago, but the discovery of your husband's addiction has opened them up again. It may be that some of the pain you are experiencing stems from old wounds, but the impact of the porn addiction is masking the other pain. As a result, you are quick to believe that your husband's choices are the source of *all* of your current suffering.

It can be difficult to separate new pain from that of old wounds, but it's important to give due diligence to this exercise. It is one thing to name past traumas or a series of trials you have experienced. It is quite another to identify and take responsibility for the ways your own sin has colored your reaction to those events. Have sin and self-righteousness caused you to judge, condemn, and resent those who hurt you? When you recognize those old wounds, it is essential to look into your defiled heart (don't be offended, we all have sinful hearts) and take responsibility for the times you have responded to painful events with an unforgiving spirit, bitterness, anger, self-righteousness, or defensiveness.

A. List what you believe to be your current wounds that have resulted from your husband's addiction to pornography and the choices he has made.

B. If you can, describe past traumas or situations that resulted in wounds that still exist today but are unrelated to your husband's addiction to porn.

How might wounds from categories A and B intermingle or confuse the source of pain?

Read Luke 1:46–55 in your Bible.

In some Bible versions, this passage is called "Mary's Magnificat." *Magnificat* is the first word of Mary's song in Latin. The phrase translates as "My soul doth magnify the Lord."

There are a few significant lessons we can take away from this passage.

- Mary's song is filled with Old Testament references because her heart and mind were saturated in God's Word.

  The take-away: You must immerse yourself in the Word of God.

- Mary expresses confidence in God's power, mercy, and faithfulness as she recites his covenant promises.

  The take-away: You must believe that God's power, mercy, faithfulness, and commitment to fulfill promises are still true for you today.

- Mary knew God as her Savior and had a relationship with him.

  The take-away: You must know Christ as your Savior.

- Mary exuded humility.

  The take-away: You must not be self-righteous. You must be broken and repentant.

When you look in the magnified mirror at your heart and mind, what do you see? Does your soul magnify the Lord?

You have done some hard work here. Well done! I want you to take it a little further in your journal. In the next chapter, we will consider how to take your brokenness to the One who will heal you.

I know, my God, that you test the heart and have pleasure in uprightness. In the uprightness of my heart I have freely offered all these things . . . . (1 Chronicles 29:17)

Journal Assignment:

If you have identified sin issues or past hurts that are festering anew, you may need to linger here a while longer. This may be especially true if you have experienced a series of traumas in your life—hurt upon hurt. Take as much time as necessary to process those past traumas and the wounds they have left.

In your journal, you might consider making a plan for confronting your past hurts. Here are some ideas to get you started.

I am willing to stop denying the pain I experienced when . . .

In the experience that caused me pain, I needed but didn't get . . .

Because of my past hurts, I tend to continue self-destructive behaviors like . . .

I am willing to do the following things in order to experience healing from old wounds . . .

Day 3: Pick It Up to Lay It Down

Sam really is a tremendous man of God. One sin that I now see in myself, which I hadn't even realized had developed over the years, was that I made the mistake of putting Sam on a pedestal. I have always admired his biblical knowledge and have relied on *his* knowledge instead of studying God's Word for myself. Sam is very scholarly and I'm relational, and I somehow felt that my relational interpretation of Scripture was not good enough. Who was my faith in—Sam or God? My identity had somehow become more tied to Sam than to who I am in Christ. So when his sin cost him his job, I wasn't sure who I was anymore. I was not the wife of a highly successful attorney or a respected man of God. I was married to a sinner whose sin was even known by leaders in the church.

—Nora

As my husband and I were dealing with this struggle, I became more and more upset that he wasn't able to control this sin. I thought to myself that certainly I am immune to such awful sin. I have never participated in any kind of pornography or sexual sin, but God definitely showed me that I am no piece of perfection, and I too can fall into sin that I don't think I am capable of doing.

—Natalie

I can think of a number of scenarios in which you need to pick up something so that you can lay it down in its rightful place. When my sons' bedroom floor is littered with laundry, I will ask them to pick up what is theirs and put it in the hamper or in the closet. Dirty dishes left anywhere but in the dishwasher need to be claimed, picked up, and put where they belong. Likewise, there are times when I have identified my sin but I haven't taken the responsible step of owning it, demonstrating remorse for it, and laying it down at the foot of the cross where it belongs.

Sometimes you have to pick it up to lay it down.

Poet Antonio Porchia wrote, "A door opens to me. I go in and am faced with a hundred closed doors."[1] To be honest, there are times when the thought of dealing with a character issue or a sin is paralyzing. I know that when I pick it up, I'm going to discover many other sins buried beneath it that will require my attention. Instead, I will observe the sin from a safe distance for a time. I may even be so bold as to name it, but not until I reach down and pick it up do I *own* it. Then and only then can I do something constructive about it.

We can talk endlessly about sin and never really do anything with it. In the last chapter I asked you to identify areas of sin in your life that may prevent you from having a soul that magnifies the Lord. When you recognize that your husband is not all bad and you are not all good and that, in fact, you have some character issues that are unacceptable in a daughter of Christ, then you're in a position to begin dealing with your own need for repentance.

Gary Thomas wrote, "I have a theory: Behind virtually every case of marital dissatisfaction lies unrepented sin. Couples don't fall out of love so much as they fall out of repentance. Sin, wrong attitudes, and personal failures that are not dealt with slowly erode the relationship, assaulting and eventually erasing the once lofty promises made in the throes of an earlier (and less polluted) passion."[2]

In the last chapter, we examined our hearts in a magnified mirror. Why a magnified mirror and not a magnifying glass? Don't we already have a tendency to wield an invisible magnifying glass? Through it, we identify and judge all the ways others have sinned against us—especially our husbands. Here's the honest truth though: Try as you might, you will never successfully judge your marriage into restoration.

What is your motive when you spend more time identifying your husband's faults than recognizing and contending with your own wrongdoing (perhaps toward your husband)?

We have addressed motives in previous chapters, but it's so important to be aware of them. Motives tend to govern the way we react toward those we encounter. It's all about our defiled hearts. When Jesus taught about food laws and ceremonial cleanliness, he demonstrated that he was most concerned with this vessel—the heart—because it is the source of all we say and do.

> For from within, out of the heart of man, come evil thoughts, sexual immorality, theft, murder, adultery, coveting, wickedness, deceit, sensuality, envy, slander, pride, foolishness. All these evil things come from within, and they defile a person. (Mark 7:21–23)

It might be very difficult to admit this, but if your husband has taken responsibility for his addiction and has shown sincere remorse, he may be better able to walk in freedom from his pornography addiction than from your disapproval and judgment. I'm just asking you to think about it.

Being honest is a form of repentance. Taking responsibility for your past behaviors, mind-sets, and choices is an essential step in spiritual healing. Naming your sins and wounds as you did in the last chapter is essential.

The next step is confessing those sins to God. I know firsthand the temptation to "explain," deny, or attempt to dress up my sins to make them appear more respectable. This is not the time for that nonsense. This is the time to agree with God that he is absolutely right and our behavior has been wholly wrong. Period. Simple as that. No excuses. No denial. You need to empty the garbage from every single emotional pocket you've got and surrender it into the hands of the Almighty. When you do, God will forgive and restore you.

This morning in my Bible study I read about the downward spiral to which one small act of sin can lead. I read about Jonah in Jonah 1, the Prodigal Son in Luke 15, and David in 2 Samuel 11. Do you remember David's story? He was loitering on his rooftop while all the other men were in battle. From his high-rise vantage point, he spied Bathsheba taking a bath and sent a messenger for her. After lying with him, Bathsheba found herself pregnant. David proceeded to make one unbelievably sinful decision after another (That's how it goes, isn't it? One sin often leads to another?) until Bathsheba's husband was killed, and David married her. Then the Lord sent the prophet Nathan to rebuke David. Psalm 51 was David's heart cry after he heard from the Lord through Nathan.

Read Psalm 51:1–17 in your Bible. This penitential psalm walks through the steps of repentance and God's forgiveness and restoration. When you read David's plea, I encourage you to write your own plea in the right-hand column.

Honestly Admit Need for Forgiveness

Have mercy on me, O God,
    according to your steadfast love;

according to your abundant mercy
    blot out my transgressions.
Wash me thoroughly from my iniquity,
    and cleanse me from my sin!

Specifically Confess and Surrender Sins and Wounds

For I know my transgressions,
    and my sin is ever before me.
Against you, you only, have I sinned
    and done what is evil in your sight,
so that you may be justified in your words
    and blameless in your judgment.
Behold, I was brought forth in iniquity,
    and in sin did my mother conceive me.
Behold, you delight in truth in the inward being,
    and you teach me wisdom in the secret heart.

Pray for Cleansing that Results in Healing

Purge me with hyssop, and I shall be clean;
    wash me, and I shall be whiter than snow.
Let me hear joy and gladness;
    let the bones that you have broken rejoice.
Hide your face from my sins,
    and blot out all my iniquities.
Create in me a clean heart, O God,
    and renew a right spirit within me.
Cast me not away from your presence,
    and take not your Holy Spirit from me.
Restore to me the joy of your salvation,
    and uphold me with a willing spirit.

Tell God How You'll Make Your Past Suffering the Starting Point of Your Service to Him

Then I will teach transgressors your ways,
    and sinners will return to you.

Deliver me from bloodguiltiness, O God,
   O God of my salvation,
   and my tongue will sing aloud of your righteousness.
O Lord, open my lips,
   and my mouth will declare your praise.
For you will not delight in sacrifice, or I would give it;
   you will not be pleased with a burnt offering.
The sacrifices of God are a broken spirit;
   a broken and contrite heart, O God, you will not despise.

Your work here is not done. When I was going through my divorce, I found myself *daily* confessing my doubt that God was going to handle all the details. Every time I went to my mailbox, it seemed I encountered something devastating: a bill from my attorney, a letter from the courts, or a hurtful letter from my soon-to-be ex-husband. Now the truth is that I was getting bad news maybe once a week; it wasn't *every* day. Nevertheless, I conditioned myself to have a fear response each time I walked to the mailbox and pulled open that little black door. Every day I found myself with my fingers curled around the mailbox knob, asking God to be my All-in-All, to forgive me for my lack of faith, to give me the strength to face whatever was inside.

I wish I could tell you that you will lay down what you picked up, took responsibility for, and asked God to forgive, and that you will leave it there, but you and I both know better. You will more than likely pick it back up again. Seeking forgiveness must be a daily exercise. It takes courage to face our sin and brokenness day after day, but when we do, we are able to move toward the One who has the resources to see us through.

The broken person . . . will find that all of the resources
of heaven and all of the Spirit's power
are now at his disposal and, unless heaven's riches can be
exhausted or the Spirit's power can be found wanting,
he cannot come up short.[3]

There is one more thing—and you need to listen carefully here. If you don't change your heart *and* your behavior, you're going to end up revisiting these sins in short order. For instance, suppose you recognize that you tend to be ruthlessly sarcastic when you speak to your husband. In your heart you have justified this disrespect for a long time, but now the Holy Spirit has spoken to your heart, telling you it's time to lay it down. So you ask God to forgive you for willfully disobeying his command to respect your man. You ask him to prick your conscience if you are ever tempted to resume this old habit. In your heart you are sincere, but if you don't actually exercise kind, respectful communication (that is, enact a behavior change), then you're going to sin again in no time. The inverse is also true. If you make a behavior change, but your heart isn't in it, you'll also fall again.

You can't heal your own tendency to sin, but you can yield it to God in repentance. You can trust that when you take responsibility for your sins and place them in the hands of the Healer, he will offer full restoration. If you think about it, it's really your only option. What are you waiting for?

Each person is tempted when he is lured and enticed by his
    own desire.
Then desire when it has conceived gives birth to sin, and sin
    when it is fully grown brings forth death.
Do not be deceived, my beloved brothers.
Every good gift and every perfect gift is from above, coming
    down from the Father of lights with whom there is no
    variation or shadow due to change.
Of his own will he brought us forth by the word of truth,
    that we should be a kind of firstfruits of his creatures.
    (James 1:14–18)

Day 4: Go Through It or Grow Through It

I needed to remind myself of the positives in my husband instead of focusing on the negatives. Personalizing my husband's sin until it became my own was so counterproductive. I'm better off allowing God to work on me, making me the best I can be so I can be a better *support* to my husband.

—Stacy

I had a choice: I could be a victim or I could be a victor. I chose to find my victory in Christ and hold it close, especially on the darkest days.

—Nicole

Dealing with one's own sin issues results in voluntary brokenness or a contrite heart, but dealing with the ramifications of a husband's addiction to pornography, lust, or masturbation slaps a woman with involuntary brokenness of her heart. You must choose if you're going to live as a victim or in victory.

I'm telling you, I know how to throw a rip-roaring pity party! Put on your favorite gray sweat suit, grab a quart of Ben & Jerry's, and prepare to do the B.E.D. boogie—blame, excuses, and denial. There was a time when I could have been a party planner for other wives of porn addicts because I had it down to a science. The problem is that pity parties are not well attended by others. In fact, they are usually a party of one. My pity parties came to a halt when I joined a secular support group. It's not that I learned better coping skills, though they tried to teach such things. No, I looked around at the other participants, none of whom seemed to know Jesus, and I realized that many of them had earned lifetime memberships to the Pity Party Club. They had no hope. These women were toxic to one another. Like yeast poured into warm water, salt, and flour, they fed each other's negativity. That's where the metaphor breaks down, however, because unlike fresh baked bread, these people produced nothing worth savoring.

I remember coming home from the support group one night, dropping onto the couch, and asking aloud, "Lord, is that really what it looks like to get better? In my opinion, they all seem happy to wear name tags that say 'Bitter.' I want something more. I don't want to go through all of this and end up bitter. I want to end up better than when I started."

How about you? Have you ever known anyone who seems content to be a pit-dweller? Who is always blaming, making excuses, or in denial? Who emulates Eeyore with a low, hovering storm cloud that pours down bitterness and gloom? Who lives life as a victim? Does she bear any resemblance to the face that's reflected in your bathroom mirror? I hope not. You have the same choice that I did. You can either choose to *go* through this experience or you can *grow* through it.

In John 5:6 at the healing pool of Bethesda, Jesus asked the invalid who had been there thirty-eight years, "Do you want to be healed?" He had a choice. So do you. Choose your role. Victor or victim? Better or bitter? Grow through it or go through it.

You can demonstrate a healthy, holy response and mature in your faith as a result of circumstances you would never have chosen. Believe it. I do. Do you see me in the front row of your cheering section? Do you hear me singing *Victory Chant* through the bullhorn? Do you have any idea how often I drop to my knees on your behalf?

To grow through the experience of being married to a porn addict and come out victorious on the other side, you need to make up your mind about a few things.

- You need to make up your mind to seek solitude.
- You need to make up your mind that God is the sole source of your identity and that you belong to him.
- You need to make up your mind to be thankful.
- You need to make up your mind not to look back with regret or guilt.

Let's dive into each of these, beginning with a reflection from Henri Nouwen.

Solitude is the furnace of transformation. Without solitude we remain victims of our society and continue to be entangled in the illusions of the false self. Jesus himself entered into this furnace. There he was tempted with the three compulsions of the world: to be relevant ("Turn stones into loaves"), to be spectacular ("Throw yourself down"), and to be powerful ("I will give you all these kingdoms"). There he affirmed God as the *only source of his identity* ("You *must* worship the Lord your God and serve him alone"). Solitude is the place of the great struggle and the great encounter—the struggle against the compulsions of the false self, and the encounter with the loving God who offers himself as the substance of the new self.[1]

You need to make up your mind to *seek* solitude, because it will not seek you. Especially now, you need to let your knees buckle and give yourself over to his Word, his throne, his grace, and his glory. Accept his offer of solitude in the midst of the tumult. This is a forging place where he will heat and reform your soul. Margaret

Clarkson observed, "If there is one thing that pain, rightly used, will do for us, it is to increase our capacity for God; and the greater our capacity for him, the more fully we shall be filled with him, and surely the more greatly we shall one day 'glorify God and enjoy Him forever.' "[2]

Solitude is where you are mindful about meeting Jesus. Just Jesus. Your heart, mind, and soul are fixed on him alone, not on your present circumstances. Here you expose your fresh, open wounds to the healing balm of the Healer. You don't deny the difficulties and pain, but you refuse to give in to their power. When you enter into solitude, you allow your thirsty soul to experience deep communion with the Living Water. He satisfies and fills you as only he can. Then he takes your malleable soul and shapes you into his image.

Write your name in the circle below. Then around the outside of the circle list actions you will need to do/not do in order to intentionally seek solitude with Jesus. (For instance, list every random thought that comes to mind when I'm praying so I can deal with it later, block off time on my calendar, and so on.)

In solitude with
Jesus

You need to make up your mind that God is the sole source of your identity and you belong to him. When you have experienced involuntary heartbreak, it's not uncommon to allow feelings of defeat to overcome you. If you aren't careful, you can convince yourself that life will always be difficult and painful because God has abandoned you. This lie gives Satan the upper hand.

Read Deuteronomy 4:31:

> For the LORD your God is a merciful God.
> He will not leave you or destroy you
> or forget the covenant with your fathers that
> he swore to them.

Our God is good. He offers you a firm place to stand. "He drew me up from the pit of destruction, out of the miry bog, and set my feet upon a rock, making my steps secure" (Psalm 40:2). Choose to believe that he is protective of you. He is for you. He believes in you. He will not fail you. He will give you strength as well as rest. He loves you and longs for you to walk in victory with him—not just for a little while, but forever. You are his witness to faith in the midst of your suffering and sacrifice. These are some of the things he wants you to know for certain.

Have you ever met someone who was cordial but clearly not open to a new friendship—leaving you just going through the motions of relating? You can do the same thing to God. You can go through the motions of meeting with him, but not demonstrate a heart response or an openness to his work in your life.

How would you describe your willingness to accept God's working in your life, to trust that you are his no matter what happens?

If you are to grow through this experience, you must persevere through the pain until you find its purpose. There you will also find healing. You are his child, and nothing will ever separate you from his love.

Read Romans 8:37–39:

> No, in all these things we are more than conquerors through
>   him who loved us.
> For I am sure that neither death nor life, nor angels nor rulers,
> nor things present nor things to come, nor powers, nor height
>   nor depth,
> nor anything else in all creation, will be able to separate us
>   from the love of God in Christ Jesus our Lord.

Do you believe that God has something for you to learn in this trial? If so, are you willing to look for what that might be? If you already have some idea of what he is teaching you, describe it here.

As you begin to recognize the lessons he has for you, make up your mind to be thankful. Yes, thankful. Don't worry, thankfulness does not minimize your pain; it magnifies the positive. Gratitude is a humble attitude of genuine faith.

I recently discovered a daily devotional that converts Scripture to read as if Jesus is speaking directly to the reader. The following is what I read:

> When you are plagued by a persistent problem—one that goes on and on—view it as a rich opportunity. An ongoing problem is like a tutor who is always by your side. The learning possibilities are limited only by your willingness to be teachable. In faith, thank

me for your problem. Ask me to open your eyes and your heart to all that I am accomplishing through this difficulty. Once you have become grateful for a problem, it loses its power to drag you down. On the contrary, your thankful attitude will lift you up into heavenly places with me. From this perspective, your difficulty can be seen as a *slight, temporary distress that is producing for you a transcendent Glory never to cease!* (Isaiah 30:20–21; 2 Corinthians 4:17)[3]

Take a few moments to ask Jesus to speak specifically to you from this devotional. Reread it and underline the messages that most resonate in your heart.

Have you been reluctant to identify things you might be thankful for regarding your husband's choices because you feared it would negate your suffering?

Your pain is very real. You can be honest about that reality without letting it blot out the many blessings God gives you every single day.

What are you grateful for today?

What are you thankful for regarding your husband?

Finally, you need to make up your mind not to look back with regret or guilt after repentance. Growing through this experience is a forward, upward movement. It is an ascent. Wherever you are right now is not where you will be when this is all over. Cling to the truth that you are just passing through, and commit yourself not to look back at past mistakes.

Read 2 Corinthians 7:10: "Godly grief produces a repentance that leads to salvation without regret, whereas worldly grief produces death."

Do I need to remind you of what happened to Lot's wife when she looked back (Genesis 19:16–26)? If God in his mercy has delivered you from past behaviors, choices, and attitudes, consider it your "Get out of Sodom free" card. Flee from the old life and don't look back!

"For freedom Christ has set us free; stand firm therefore, and do not submit again to a yoke of slavery" (Galatians 5:1). You have a choice to make. Go through it or grow through it?

> Look! It is winter, and you have come
> alone to this clearing in the wood,
> a familiar place you have never
> seen before. Do not hurry to leave,
> but when at last you turn away,
> remember this, if you remember nothing else,
> You are no longer who you were.[4]

Journal Assignment:

Complete the following prayer with your own heart cries.

Lord, help me to fight the voices of the enemy that tell me my life will be defined by . . .

I believe your love is the single, constant reality I can hold onto. Take me into solitude, the furnace of transformation, and burn off . . .

Be the sole source of my identity. May I look more like you in the way that I . . .

Remind me not to look back at _____ with regret or guilt, but to fix my eyes above my circumstances and firmly on you.

Father, I trust you to take the most painful places in my life and show me that I can be grateful for _____ without glossing over my suffering.

God, I believe you will see me through the messy process of healing, so I may grow to live better, not bitter, and be a victor, not a victim. Amen.

Day 5: A New Mosaic

God has taught me that the people I love the most can bring tragic, life-sucking pain into my guts. When it happens, it's best to take your guts to God where he can put you back together again. I don't know how he does it; I just know he does.

—Olivia

mo·sa·ic [mō záy ik] *n*: a picture or design made with small pieces of colored material such as glass or tile stuck onto a surface.[1]

In the end, life breaks us all, but you can become stronger in the broken places if you are committed to put the pieces back together with God's help. Your life, as you emerge on the other side of this life experience, has the potential to be breathtaking.

I vividly remember sitting in the pew of our small church A.P. (After Pornography—in those days everything about my life was categorized B.P. or A.P. Photographs record the date in my eyes.) The pastor was teaching through the book of James, and he simply said, "Pray for trials."

Tears brimmed. Gut twisted. Chest squeezed. Knowing eyes turned in my direction. I mouthed, "I don't think so."

I couldn't imagine asking God to allow me to experience the kind of suffering I was already enduring. Wasn't my heart broken into enough fragments? My marriage vows were fractured. My dreams were crushed. My self-esteem was torn. My trust was shattered. I had nothing left to offer up for demolition.

My eyes dropped to my worn Bible and a highlighted promise that had soothed my wounded spirit in days past: "Count it all joy, my brothers, when you meet trials of various kinds, for you know that the testing of your faith produces steadfastness. And let steadfastness have its full effect, *that you may be perfect and complete*, lacking in nothing" (James 1:2–4, italics mine). Hard to believe, but there it was, and in the narrow margins of my trusted friend, I found an admonition written to myself: *Jesus learned things through his suffering. So must I.*

There is something to be said for the hardest, most painful, gut-wrenching times in our lives. It is there, in the dark nights of the soul, that Christ meets us. He picks up the pieces of our heart and heals the wounds. Wounds of the heart, of the soul, of the spirit—he puts the pieces together in such a way that we are never quite the same as we were before he touched our most vulnerable places. He creates a new mosaic—a life unimaginable.

> Blessed is the man who remains steadfast under trial,
> for when he has stood the test, he will receive the crown of life,
> which God has promised to those who love him. (James 1:12)

I am convinced that God has a plan for your life, and it's good. He can't be anything but good. Do you believe it?

If you believe God has a good plan for your life (even if you can't imagine it now), tell him. Write a *simple* prayer here, one that might echo in your heart to a rhythm that soothes your soul.

I am no artist. I can create things with words all right, but given clay, chalk, metals, wood, fabric, crayons, or any other artistic tool, I'm a bust. In junior high art class I muddled through a unit on clay and sculpting. To this day my family teases me about the gray, legless hippopotamus sporting fuchsia lips that I created. It started out as a horse that became a pig and somehow morphed into a hippo. (Don't ask.) For whatever reason, my mom held onto this treasure. I would like to think she did this to remind me that God can turn something ugly into something beautiful just as I did, but if you ever saw my hippo, you'd know I was trying to pull a fast one. Nevertheless, even though I can't, God can.

God has a redemptive work in mind for you. Isaiah 64:8 says, "But now, O LORD, you are our Father; we are the clay, and you are the potter; we are all the work of your hand." Sometimes clay is flawed. The flaw is not a reflection of the potter's skill. But a skillful potter can see the potential of the pliable (though flawed) material he holds in his hands, so he redeems it and shapes it into something beautiful.

Read Jeremiah 18:4: "And the vessel he was making of clay was spoiled in the potter's hand, and he reworked it into another vessel, as it seemed good to the potter to do."

How might this passage apply to your current circumstances?

I don't have to tell you what happens after the clay is shaped, do I? It gets fired. Wouldn't it be nice to escape when life gets hot—when it feels like you're living in a pressure cooker? A pressure cooker is "a heavy cooking pot with an airtight lid: a specially designed pot used to steam food at high pressure, at a higher temperature and in a shorter time than by boiling."[2] It's a very efficient way to cook food quickly.

Since the first day intuition whispered in your ear that something wasn't right in your marriage, since the moment your husband confessed or you fell upon his obsession with pornography, you have been living in a pressure cooker. While it may be tempting to try to escape and live in denial with your eyes squeezed shut, it will only slow down the redemptive work of the Refiner's fire.

Complete this thought: His redemptive work is done faster in me if I temporarily live in a pressure cooker, so I will . . .

Read Isaiah 48:10: "Behold, I have refined you, but not as silver; I have tried you in the furnace of affliction."

This passage moves us away from clay toward silver, but we are still being refined in the fire, removing impurities in order to produce a purer form of what God intends us to be. Sometimes it seems that we have been in the fire too long. Is it possible to ensure that we are refined but not destroyed by the Refiner's fire?

Read Malachi 3:1–6.

When the Lord comes, he will purify some sinners and judge others. Malachi says ". . . he is like a refiner's fire and like fullers' soap" (3:2b). Both are means of ridding one of filth, that is, sin. We qualify for refining (the burning up of our sin) rather than devastation when we put our trust in God's purifying mercy. "For behold, the day is coming, burning like an oven . . . . But for you who fear my name, the sun of righteousness shall rise with healing in its wings" (Malachi 4:1a, 2).

Trust him. Don't give in to the impulse to leap out of the refining fire and hide because God has a work to do in this hot spot. Stay in the pressure cooker until he declares you "well done." After all, he is an expert in the business of refining.

Living in the pressure cooker may mean different things to different women. It may mean you quit denying prickly, uncomfortable feelings and deal with them. Maybe you seek counseling or commit yourself to difficult conversations with your husband. The pressure cooker may mean that you set boundaries with your husband and follow through with prearranged consequences if the boundaries aren't honored. (For instance, you establish the boundary that if he stays out all night again, you will need a separation from him until he seeks counseling and demonstrates a desire and effort to make changes.) Perhaps the pressure cooker means that you take a hard look at issues you still need to address in your own character.

Christ will use your time in the Refiner's fire to weld together the pieces of your heart. Spiritual healing *in the midst of* your husband's addiction is possible only because heat is required to fuse the pieces of your heart back together into a new mosaic.

There are two things you must do when you're living in the Refiner's fire. First, you must *release* anyone from your grudge. "And whenever you stand praying, forgive, if you have anything against anyone, so that your Father also who is in heaven may forgive you your trespasses" (Mark 11:25). I have intentionally not addressed the issue of forgiving your husband until now. That does not minimize its importance. Forgiveness is an essential piece of business while you are in the fire, so I will address this at length in the following chapters.

Second, you need to refocus your attention on the beautiful work God is doing—even when you can't see it yet—rather than on the flames licking your heart. "Now to him who is able to do far more abundantly than all that we ask or think, according to the power at work within us, to him be glory in the church and in

Christ Jesus throughout all generations, forever and ever. Amen" (Ephesians 3:20–21).

Remember, God doesn't change, so you will not be destroyed (Malachi 3:6). Now is the time for you to demonstrate an unshakeable confidence that God's love and faithfulness are steadfast. He has a spectacular mosaic in mind for your heart and your life. It may not be what you had envisioned when you said "I do." However, it will be a priceless piece of art in his eyes.

I need to be honest with you. Where you are in the healing process will determine how easy it is to hear and accept the things you have read in this chapter (and in the chapters to come). Let's say you only recently discovered your husband's addiction, and this book is the first place you turned. You may have some grieving and other healing to do before you can accept the idea of God creating something beautiful out of this disaster. It's okay. Don't rush it. Meditate on the truths presented here and then cycle through them again when you're further along in the healing of your broken heart. His timing is perfect.

It may be that you have been on this journey for a long time now, and your husband is a "sober porn addict." If that's the case, it will be easier for you to see where you've been and compare it to where you are now in your personal healing and in the healing of your marriage.

Then again, your husband may not have accepted responsibility for his addiction or made any effort to recover. If that's your situation, you may still be in the thick of the chaos, or perhaps you are separated or divorced. Again, this will determine your ability to recognize the transformed, reconstructed heart mosaic God is creating.

To the best of your ability, list points of contrast between your life before/during the pornography and after/in the midst of healing. If you are still in the thick of things, you may describe what you hope will be your heart's design when you are on the other side of this. (I'll get you started.)

Old Heart/Life	New Mosaic
Avoided discussing my needs.	I share my needs, knowing that my husband can't always meet them, but God can.
I was suspicious, nagging, and judgmental.	We trust each other to be honest, always.

A silversmith fixes his eye on the furnace to ensure that his precious silver isn't damaged, but rather purified to the point that his image is reflected in it. In the same way, Christ has not taken his eyes off you. He will make certain that you are not consumed by the flames of affliction, but purified so that his image is reflected in your heart.

> In this you rejoice, though now for a little while, if necessary, you have been grieved by various trials, so that the tested genuineness of your faith—more precious than gold that perishes though it is tested by fire—may be found to result in praise and glory and honor at the revelation of Jesus Christ. (1 Peter 1:6–7)

FORGIVENESS

WEEK 6

Day 1: A Choice

I have learned that forgiveness is a choice and not a feeling. I have learned that it does not excuse what was done. I know that unforgiveness is like a prison and that harboring feelings of ill will toward anyone only hurts me . . . the other person goes on with life one way or another, while I am keeping the memory of the wrongdoing alive. I believe that unforgiveness is a sin itself. How can I expect God to forgive me of so much when I can't forgive others?

—Dianna

Forgiveness is a choice I have had to make, and Scripture tells me it is a must. I have to remember, sometimes daily, how many times God has forgiven me. That helps me to forgive my husband over and over again—not just about his sexual addiction, but for other things. Plus it helps me to forgive myself and all my inadequacies.

—Nora

Don't skip this chapter!

Please keep reading. Regardless of where you are in the journey of your broken heart, I believe you will learn things here that surprise you—things that will significantly impact your spiritual healing.

You have probably figured out that this chapter is about forgiveness. There was a time in my own journey when rage would boil like a smoldering volcano at the thought that I should forgive my husband. I think that's normal.

You have been hurt more deeply than you ever dreamed possible. In the core of your being you have wondered if you can ever forgive your husband. At the same time you know God's Word instructs you to forgive. Therein lies the tension.

Before we proceed, I must ask whether it is possible that your husband isn't the only one you need to forgive. It's not surprising that you may need to consider forgiving your husband, but have you considered whether there are others you haven't forgiven?

Take a moment to ask God to bring to mind everyone you may need to forgive. Then list each person who comes to mind. Don't concern yourself right now about whether or not you need to forgive them or why you might need to extend forgiveness. Simply list any names the Holy Spirit places on your heart.

Do you need to include yourself on that list?

Throughout this book I have told you that your husband's addiction to porn, lust, and self-gratification is not your fault. Nonetheless, perhaps you still blame yourself for ways you believe you contributed to your husband's struggle. Releasing your self-condemnation is essential to your healing process. Acknowledging *all* who have let you down, including yourself and possibly (in your mind) God, is an important step in your healing.

God's love for you was confirmed on the cross. Even so, some women in your situation find that they harbor negative feelings toward him for not coming to their rescue, for not sheltering them from this heartache, and for not answering their cries in the night. Is it possible that you are one of them?

God does not need you to forgive him, for he can do no wrong. However, if you pour out your disappointments to him and ask him to help you in that struggle, you will strengthen your relationship with him. Don't wait. Tell him right now.

Now let's zoom in on the topic of forgiving your husband. Would God really instruct you to forgive a man who has broken his vows? Must you forgive your husband if he continues his use of pornography and other sexually immoral choices? Even if he does not acknowledge the damage he's done in your marriage, let alone ask for forgiveness?

What if I told you that the answer to the first question is a conditional yes, and the answer to the second and third questions is no? Now are you willing to continue reading? I thought so.

Many evangelical churches routinely teach and preach that "unconditional forgiveness" is a biblical requirement. After much study, I don't believe that to be the case. Extending unconditional forgiveness to unrepentant sinners undermines the gospel of Jesus Christ and deprives Christ of his due glory. Dietrich Bonhoeffer wrote, "Cheap grace is the preaching of forgiveness without requiring repentance . . . absolution without personal confession."[1]

Read 1 John 1:9: "If we confess our sins, he is faithful and just to forgive us our sins and to cleanse us from all unrighteousness."

According to this passage, God is faithful and just and will forgive us our sins *if* _____.

Listen carefully. If God forgives the sins of those who *refuse* to confess and repent, he nullifies the power of the cross. He rescinds Christ's sacrifice of death. Forgiveness does not happen without confession *and* repentance.

We are to imitate Christ (1 Corinthians 11:1), which means we are to forgive as he forgives. He extends grace and mercy, forgiving *those who repent,* and so must we. "[Bear] with one another and, if one has a complaint against another, [forgive] each other, *as the Lord has forgiven you*" (Colossians 3:13, italics mine). Ardel B. Caneday writes:

> Therefore, if we profligately grant forgiveness even though the person who sinned against us remains unrepentant, we reveal little sense of the magnitude or gravity of sin's offense to God, we trample underfoot the dignity of the cross, we cheapen the grace of God revealed in Christ, we proclaim the fiendish fiction that divine and human forgiveness is unconditional, we show little understanding of the correlation of human and divine forgiveness, and we actually impede the sinner's repentance and remission of sin because we eliminate an incentive of guilt the gospel inflicts upon the unrepentant.[2]

Let me put this as simply as I can. If your husband is still looking at porn on the computer, renting X-rated movies, or engaging in other sexually immoral activities without owning his choices, repenting of them, or taking sincere steps to stop his behavior, *then you are under no obligation to extend forgiveness.* Forgiving him when he is unrepentant minimizes the damage he has done to your marriage and to you personally. Forgiving him when he is still actively pursuing his addiction interferes with his need to repent and seek restoration from God, which will have eternal consequences.

If your husband is still engaging in sexual immorality, has not accepted responsibility for his sin, and is unrepentant, then forgiving him would mean doing what God himself will not do.

> I have always been a very forgiving person—even to my own detriment because I forgave when it wasn't even asked for. I do it for myself, to free my own heart. What I am learning, though, is that if you still want to maintain the relationship, there must be genuine repentance and changed behavior. Trust, I believe, is earned through a repentant heart, sorrow for the pain you have caused to another, and most of all by changed behavior.
>
> —Sarah

There is another side to this coin. Though forgiving may feel unmerited, undeserved, and uncomfortable, *if* the offender has repented and sought forgiveness from you, it is essential to *your* spiritual health to grant it. It is not your husband, your in-laws, your husband's past or present friends, or anyone else who is getting their just deserts by your decision to hold them in bondage to their sin. Your lack of forgiveness is not causing them to pay for the hurt they have caused you. You don't have that kind of power over anyone. *You* are the one who suffers. *You* are the one in bondage.

> For if you forgive others their trespasses, your heavenly Father will also forgive you, but if you do not forgive others their trespasses, neither will your Father forgive your trespasses. (Matthew 6:14–15)

221

Where does this leave you? Take a moment and consider whether you *do* need to grant forgiveness, based on your husband's confession and repentance, or *do not*, based on his nonconfession and lack of repentance.

"We are all living with the consequences of someone else's sin."[3]

Let's be honest: that stinks. My flesh insists it is simply not fair for the fallout of life to injure an innocent bystander! *This was not my choice—it was my husband's!* Can you relate?

You are living with the consequences of your husband's sin. That's the reality. His choices were not yours, yet you experience the repercussions. *Now* is when you have a choice. Assuming your husband has repented and sought forgiveness, the ball is now in your court. Forgiveness is your choice; it's a decision of the will.

Is that you I hear screaming "But I'm not ready to forgive him"? There are various reasons why we choose to withhold forgiveness. It may be that *your wounds are simply too fresh* and the idea of forgiving is unfathomable. If your awareness of your husband's addiction is brand new, please do not feel pressured to forgive quickly. I'll address this more in Week 6 Day 3, but suffice it to say, forgiveness is a process. Keep reading, but know that a time will come, not too far down the road, when you will read this chapter again. Ask Jesus to tell you when it is time to move forward with forgiveness.

Perhaps you believe that a refusal to forgive *will protect you from further pain.* This is especially likely if you think that forgiving your husband somehow condones his choices, good or bad, and lets him off the moral hook.

Day 1: A Choice

Let me do all I can to assure you that forgiving your man is *not* the same as condoning his past, present, or future choices. Forgiveness frees *you* to release your husband to the only One who can bring about transformational changes in his heart and life.

God. Knows. What. Sin. Has. Been. Done. Trust him to deal with your husband according to his righteousness, not your bitterness.

I suspect that one reason you may allow an unforgiving spirit to linger is because *you don't feel like forgiving* just yet. Guess what? You need to get over that. You may never feel like forgiving your husband. That's a fact. If you wait until you have a strong desire to forgive, you may one day stand before Jesus with a serious problem to explain. (Note: Matthew 18:21–35 tells a sobering story about an unforgiving servant and what happens when we choose that path. Check it out.) The enemy rejoices and his minions throw a party when one of God's children won't forgive. If your husband has genuinely repented, you have an obligation to forgive. When you do, God untangles you from the things you hate most and heals your heart.

A refusal to forgive settles down in your heart when *you think forgiving your husband means trusting him as well*. It does not. Undeserved forgiveness makes you look like Jesus, but unearned trust makes you look like a fool.

Sometimes we make the mistake of thinking it's okay to withhold forgiveness as long as we're withholding it for the right reasons. Nothing could be further from the truth. Dallas Willard writes the following:

> We must beware of believing that it is okay for us to condemn as long as we are condemning the right things. It is not so simple as all that. I can trust Jesus to go into the temple and drive out those who were profiting from religion, beating them with a rope. I cannot trust myself to do so.[4]

Don't miss this. We are to forgive those who repent without additional conditions, but nowhere in the Bible does it say we are to trust anyone except God himself without reason. Trust is earned by a man's character, but forgiveness is given because of God's character. That is why you should never trust another human being to the same degree that you trust God. That level of trust must be reserved for God alone.

In a previous chapter I cautioned you that rebuilding trust will probably take much longer than it will take to forgive your husband. There is no shame in saying, "I love you, I forgive you, but I need some time before I trust you."

> Now it is required that those who have been given a trust must prove faithful. (1 Corinthians 4:2 NIV)

Read Luke 23:26–43.

Notice that though Jesus was hanging on the cross (v. 33) when he said, "Father, forgive them, for they know not what they do" (v. 34), that does not mean that God mocked the atonement by unconditionally forgiving those who put Christ on the cross. To behave in a forgiving manner and to actually forgive are two different actions.

If your husband is unrepentant, then choosing not to forgive just yet does not mean you are unforgiving, holding a grudge, or bitter. A *forgiving spirit* demonstrates a willingness to grant forgiveness when the sinner repents.

You might be saying, "If I shouldn't forgive my husband because he's stubbornly unrepentant, then what am I to do with these suffocating feelings?" Stand ready to forgive, just as God stands ready to receive your husband's confession and repentance. Pray that God would move your husband to repentance so that you and God may both forgive. Hold out the promise of future forgiveness to your husband; tell him you are prepared to forgive when he owns his behavior, repents, and seeks healing for his addiction.

Eagerly anticipate opportunities to forgive, even if it's not for the pornography addiction, but for residual consequences of your husband's sin. For instance, let's say that your husband was spending money on website fees and 900 numbers. Now he has stopped and you can account for your family's money. This may be a good time to affirm his choices and forgive him for past financial difficulties related to porn.

(Take a deep breath. Exhale. This is difficult stuff, I know. Persevere.)

What might this mean in terms of your need to forgive your husband for the consequences of his sin that have splashed all over you?

If your husband has confessed and sought forgiveness from you, then forgiveness is no longer for *his* benefit. How you choose to deal with forgiveness once he repents will have eternal consequences for *you*. It is why we are told to "Let all bitterness and wrath and anger and clamor and slander be put away from you, along with all malice. Be kind to one another, tenderhearted, forgiving one another, *as* God in Christ forgave you" (Ephesians 4:31–32, italics mine). I encourage you not to be stingy with godly forgiveness.

In a perfect world, your husband would not have made the choices he made and you would not be carrying a wounded heart right now. I don't have to tell you that this is not a perfect world, and hurt is inevitable. Trouble will come. But let me remind you that Jesus said, "In the world you will have tribulation. But take heart; I have overcome the world" (John 16:33). He has a plan.

I had to trust that his love, his plan, his forgiveness—for my own individual, personal life—is greater, bigger, more profound, more personal than my brain or heart could possibly imagine, even surpassing my wildest imagination.

—Sarah

Have we thoroughly debunked all the false beliefs that have been obstacles to forgiving? I pray that we have, because an unforgiving spirit has some ugly consequences of its own. Obedience to God's command to forgive as he forgives frees you from oppression and saves you from bitter roots.

Finally, I want to assure you that *forgiving does not mean forgetting, nor does it permit vengeance.* These are such important points that I have devoted the next chapter to these truths.

Read Hebrews 12:15: "See to it that no one fails to obtain the grace of God; that no "root of bitterness" springs up and causes trouble, and by it many become defiled."

Do you see potential roots of bitterness in your life that require your attention? For instance, a bitter root might look like the following attitude: "Because of my husband's preference for porn (now or in the past), I will protect myself from being hurt by never again allowing him to touch me in sexual or nonsexual ways." Take a personal inventory and name any bitter roots that need to be dug up.

Day 1: A Choice

The choice to forgive is solely yours. You must do business with your Maker. Wrestle with him over this one if need be, but when you are done, I encourage you to go to a private place and drop to your knees. God will meet you there. When you offer grace to your husband, God will pour out his healing, restorative graces all over you. Might this result in a healing between you and your husband? Yes—as God wills it. But certainly it will result in a healing between you and your heavenly Father.

Journal Assignment:

You may not believe you have the strength or desire to forgive. That's okay; you don't have to do this alone. In fact, you can't. When the Holy Spirit directs, turn to your journal and ask God to help you forgive. This need not be limited to your husband; it may include anyone who has added to the pain of this betrayal. Then make the hard choice to forgive, knowing that soon you will celebrate unbridled joy and freedom.

I'll get you started:

Father God, I choose to forgive _____ for _____.
(Repeat for each person on the list you created at the beginning of this chapter.)

Lord, you said, "And I will give you a new heart, and a new spirit I will put within you. And I will remove the heart of stone from your flesh and give you a heart of flesh" (Ezekiel 36:26). I am believing you for this.

In the name of your Son, whose shed blood resulted in my own forgiveness. Amen.

Day 2: Not Forgetting,
but Not Vengeful

In answer to the question "What does forgiveness of your husband look like?"—grace and mercy. Giving something he does not deserve because God forgave me. Extending mercy when punishment is really deserved. However, there are still consequences for behaviors that do not belong in our marriage. I try hard to let God deliver those, and he has been very faithful.

—Jessica

Letting him off the hook. Letting go of personalizing his sin as somehow my fault. Dropping all pretenses of any one of us being perfect. Understanding the addiction process . . . knowing that he will always be an addict and that this is his favorite substance. It's his Kryptonite.

—Olivia

Not bringing it up in an argument or holding grudges. It is truly water under the bridge.

—Lynne

My daughter babysits for family friends every other Wednesday afternoon while the mother goes to work. One afternoon, six-year-old, homeschooled Annika chatted through the living room window with a neighbor girl who had just exited the school bus. Annika had recently had a tiff with her friend and had painstakingly printed and delivered a note to the little girl: "You need Jesus." On this day, Annika called out the window to her friend as she ran for home, "Choose the narrow path!"

Choosing to forgive a repentant husband *is* choosing the narrow path. It's the harder way. On this path you will learn lessons of God's grace you might not have learned otherwise. Most certainly, you will walk closely with your Savior. On this narrow path, you will experience freedom from painful feelings as you surrender them one by one.

Some Christians teach that if you don't forgive *and* forget, you have not really forgiven at all. Their apparent therapeutic theology suggests that you do not need to deal with the past if only you fix your eyes on what is to come. They will use Philippians to build their case.

Forgetting what lies behind and straining forward to what lies ahead, I press on toward the goal . . . . (Philippians 3:13b–14)

What these well-meaning Christians are missing is the fact that Paul is not talking about forgetting all of his sinful past. Instead, he learned from it and lived with it as something that was settled. This is what you must do as well.

If anyone else thinks he has reason for confidence in the flesh, I have more: circumcised on the eighth day, of the people of Israel, of the tribe of Benjamin, a Hebrew of Hebrews; as to the law, a Pharisee; as to zeal, a persecutor of the church; as to righteousness under the law, blameless. (Philippians 3:4b–6)

Forgiving does not mean forgetting, despite anything you have heard to the contrary. Forgiving your husband is not his "Get out of jail free" card. It doesn't mean you will forget his addiction ever happened and that there won't be consequences. When you forgive, you don't exchange your spyglasses for blinders.

Trust must be earned. You will still hold him accountable and ask how he is doing with his struggle. Forgiving your husband doesn't mean that those old feelings of pain and anger won't bubble to the surface ever again. They will, and when they do, you will need to work to surrender them to their rightful place—in God's hands—again. If your husband's choices led you to sleep apart for a designated period of time, please understand that forgiving him may not alter this boundary. Neither will it mean automatic reconciliation if you are separated from your husband.

Forgiveness *does* mean that you will *not* keep him indebted to you because of his wrongdoing. You will relinquish your assumed right to punish him, to wield his sin like a hidden machete, cutting him off at the knees at any hint of moral imperfection.

> Blessed are those whose lawless deeds are forgiven, and whose sins are covered; blessed is the man against whom the Lord will not count his sin. (Romans 4:7–8)

In the last chapter, I asked you to look at a passage from Colossians. Now read it in context.

> Put on then, as God's chosen ones, holy and beloved, compassionate hearts, kindness, humility, meekness, and patience, bearing with one another and, if one has a complaint against another, forgiving each other; as the Lord has forgiven you, so you also must forgive. And above all these put on love, which binds everything together in perfect harmony. (Colossians 3:12–14)

Forgiveness means choosing to love through the hurt and remembering that "love covers a multitude of sins" (1 Peter 4:8).

Take an imaginary video sample of all your interactions with your husband in the last week, month, season, or year. How does he look? How do you look? Describe the evidence you see and hear of forgiveness and a lack of forgiveness.

Forgiveness looks & sounds like:	Unforgiveness looks & sounds like:
Letting him be the head of the house without strings attached.	I'm not discreet with details of his his past betrayal.

Have you heard the passage that says, "You . . . strain out a gnat and swallow a camel!" (Matthew 23:24 NASB)? Strict Pharisees would strain their drinking water to eliminate even a gnat, the smallest unclean creature, though figuratively they would swallow an entire camel. When you are quick to identify every single one of your husband's idiosyncrasies at the same time that you compile an exhaustive list of ways to make him pay for the hurt he has caused you, you are guilty of straining a gnat but swallowing a camel.

Read Romans 12:18–19: "If possible, so far as it depends on you, live peaceably with all. Beloved, never avenge yourselves, but leave it to the wrath of God, for it is written, "Vengeance is mine, I will repay, says the Lord."

God will collect on what was taken from you. The Greek word used for "avenge" in this text is *ekdikeō* (ek-dē-ke'-ō), meaning "to punish a person for a thing or to vindicate." The believer is warned against taking retribution into his or her own hands. When God says he will avenge, he also adds that he will "repay." This sounds like a double whammy for the sinner. What's more, the Bible specifically says that he will take care of situations involving sexual immorality.

Read 1 Thessalonians 4:3–8. Note: the Greek word for "the Lord is an avenger" is *ekdikos*. (Sound familiar?) Underline phrases that assure you God has vengeance in his hands.

> For this is the will of God, your sanctification: that you abstain from sexual immorality; that each one of you know how to control his own body in holiness and honor, not in the passion of lust like the Gentiles who do not know God; that no one transgress and wrong his brother in this matter, because the Lord is an avenger in all these things, as we told you beforehand and solemnly warned you. For God has not called us for impurity, but in holiness. Therefore whoever disregards this, disregards not man but God, who gives his Holy Spirit to you.

This passage assures us that God is the one who exacts a penalty from a person who "wrongs his brother," particularly in the matter of adultery. *Brother* here means another believer. I don't have to tell you that sexual immorality harms more than the one engaging in it. God knows that when your husband lusted with his eyes and engaged in self-gratification, his sin hurt you as well.

I know that when the one you love has wronged you, it can be very difficult not to seek retribution. In fact, revenge might seem justified in your mind, and if we're being honest, sometimes it feels good.

In what ways have you found yourself considering, fantasizing about, or actually engaging in revenge for the hurt your husband's addiction has caused you?

I know many women who have spitefully sought out extramarital affairs just to make their husbands "see how it feels." I have listened as women made sexually charged comments about other men in their husband's presence. (Not that such behavior is acceptable when they are *not* in his presence either.)

The truth of the matter is that you and I are incapable of avenging ourselves without sinning. We lean toward having a heartless, retaliatory spirit when we do it. It's not pretty.

The bottom line is that as believers, we are under God's authority. If he says vengeance is his, we must yield to him any dreams or desires we have conjured up. But listen to me: your Father in heaven is just and righteous. He knows every detail about your circumstances. He even knows details you are unaware of, including the motives of the hearts involved. You can be confident that he will bring about his perfect plan for justice. And if it's his will, he will bring it about in such a way that there can be healing, restoration, and holiness.

Journal Assignment:

In Romans 12, God not only tells us not to take revenge into our own hands, he also tells us how to treat our husband so that he may come to repentance, if he hasn't already.

Read verses 17–21 below. After each verse, respond to the instruction given. I've given starters.

"Repay no one evil for evil, but give thought to do what is honorable in the sight of all" (v. 17).

As a believer, I have a high moral standard that I must not betray, so I will . . .

"If possible, so far as it depends on you, live peaceably with all" (v. 18).

As much as possible, I will demonstrate that I am a peacemaker in my marriage by . . .

"Beloved, never avenge yourselves, but leave it to the wrath of God, for it is written, 'Vengeance is mine, I will repay, says the Lord'" (v. 19).

I trust and believe that . . .

"To the contrary: 'If your enemy is hungry, feed him; if he is thirsty, give him something to drink; for by so doing you will heap burning coals on his head.' Do not be overcome by evil, but overcome evil with good" (vv. 20–21).

Instead of _____ I will _____, so that my husband's relationship with the Lord and with me may be restored.

Day 3: The Hard Truth

Forgiveness in our situation is the main component of the healing process. The initial act was forgiven, but this continually comes back up as new dips into sin occur. My husband hasn't ever asked for forgiveness from me for the repeated times after the initial one. I believe he no longer sees this as a sin against me, but a sin against God. And I am okay with that.

—Natalie

My husband never did acknowledge his sinful behavior. I could be standing behind him while the computer screen still screamed pornographic images and he would deny his addiction. I could be holding a $400 phone bill or love letters he'd received from someone other than me in his not-so-secret-anymore post office box, and he'd say I was imagining things or blowing it out of proportion. When he flew halfway around the country to meet someone he'd met online and refused to take my calls, I was forced to remove my blinders. No longer could he manipulate my thinking to make me believe I was a lunatic. At the counsel of my pastor and Christian therapist, I filed for divorce. It was, up until that point, the single hardest thing I'd ever done.

—Nicole

The nurturer in me longs to offer you a piece of gourmet chocolate or a cappuccino because we both know that a spoonful of sugar helps the medicine go down. We need to talk about some hard truths. A little truth therapy will help you gird yourself against misbeliefs. There will be no surprises here. I will address the following three hard truths in this chapter:

- Forgiving fast is not the answer.
- Your husband may slip or have a relapse.
- There may come a time when circumstances demand that you look at the viability of your marriage.

After all this talk about forgiveness, now I'm going to suggest that you may need to pull back the reins a bit. I know a young woman who caught her husband masturbating in front of the computer. When it finally registered what she was seeing, she was horrified, but the shock prevented her from experiencing the rush of feelings associated with such a discovery. Those would come later. Her husband was embarrassed and ashamed. They exchanged a few words, and he apologized profusely. Young in her faith, she knew God instructs his children to forgive, so before even leaving the room, she informed her husband that he was forgiven.

I don't know what your reaction to her choice is, but mine was one of disbelief: "Tell me she did not just do that." Forgiving fast is *not* the answer. It is essential that a woman work through the painful feelings associated with this situation. Forgiving quickly doesn't make the pain stop. Do you see how one might believe that if she says the words "I forgive you," God will spare her from the breathtaking, torturous agony she is experiencing at the moment of revelation? It's not uncommon to think—and even to say aloud— *I'll forgive you right now. You'll never do this again, and we'll both go on as if this was just a bad dream. Agreed?*

It doesn't work that way. Many times I have told you that trusting your husband may take longer than forgiving him. The surge of feelings you experience in the wake of discovery takes time to process and surrender. Some Christian men may attempt to demand forgiveness from their wives, believing it is their biblical responsibility to forgive. This type of man is also apt to believe that, like an Etch-a-Sketch, his wife's memory of his miserable choices has been turned over, shaken, and wiped clean so it's good as new. He will become accusatory, withdrawn, or annoyed when she is depressed, angry, or inquisitive.

The goal of forgiveness is healing and growth. Fast forgiveness sabotages the healthy work that needs to be done to experience genuine, long-lasting restoration.

> Dealing with sexual sin is a process and not an event. I recall one time several months after my husband told me of his struggle. We were sitting in church listening to a message on forgiveness. My husband leaned over and whispered to me that he knew he had apologized for what he had done, but he didn't remember asking me for forgiveness. He then proceeded to do that. Needless to say, I spent the morning in tears as we came yet one step closer to the ultimate healing that continues to occur. So the need never goes away, and God does seem to always have the perfect timing for meeting that need in various ways.
>
> —Natalie

In light of all the information about forgiveness that you have read thus far, do you think you have been operating under some misconceptions about forgiveness? What are they?

I sincerely pray that your husband has repented and sought help in dealing with his addiction to and compulsion for pornography. I also pray that either you are on the road to forgiveness or have worked through your feelings and found freedom in forgiveness already. If both of these are true for you (and I hope they are), then what I'm about to say may be a bitter pill to swallow. Forgiveness and healing come with no guarantees that your husband won't give in to sexual temptation again—with slips and relapses—or that your painful feelings won't bubble up in the future.

Debra Laaser writes:

What distinguishes a slip from a relapse is frequency and intensity. A slip is a short lapse in progress. For a man who has been struggling with pornography, a slip would involve visiting an Internet site after months of abstaining from any kind of sexual acting out. A slip may be a one-time occurrence, or it may just involve serious thoughts of sliding back into old behaviors. A relapse, on the other hand, is a complete return to sinful sexual behaviors and patterns. Its intensity is determined by the possible consequences of the behaviors.[1]

Sometimes repeated forgiveness is necessary when there has been a slip or your husband has genuinely repented after a relapse. That can be especially challenging. As hard as it may be, God's will is for you to forgive your husband.

Read Jesus' words in Luke 17:3–4: "If your brother sins, rebuke him, and if he repents, forgive him, and if he sins against you seven times in the day, and turns to you seven times, saying, 'I repent,' you must forgive him."

Read Matthew 18:21–35 in your Bible.

What does the passage from Luke (17:3–4) contribute to your understanding of the Matthew passage you just read?

Is there something someone could do to you that you could never forgive?

What does this parable teach about our unwillingness to forgive? How does that sit with you?

This "seventy times seven" model suggests that even with repeated slips or relapses in the same sin, we are called to forgive. (Just a reminder: God forgives us this way as well.) It can get sticky here because true repentance requires that we turn "from acts that lead to death" (Hebrews 6:1 NIV).

Read the following passages and underline the phrases that support the teaching that true repentance requires a turning from the sinful behavior.

I . . . declared . . . that they should repent and turn to God, performing deeds in keeping with their repentance. (Acts 26:19–20)

Though they know God's righteous decree that those who practice such things deserve to die, they not only do them but give approval to those who practice them. (Romans 1:32)

I fear that when I come again my God may humble me before you, and I may have to mourn over many of those who sinned earlier and have not repented of the impurity, sexual immorality, and sensuality that they have practiced. (2 Corinthians 12:21)

Sincerity is the key. Verbal repentance is empty words if it is simply a "cover" for continuously playing in the deep, dark, shark-infested waters of pornography. Sometimes it is next to impossible to tell if your husband is temporarily struggling or if he is simply unwilling to change his behaviors. Pray. Pray. And pray some more that God will reveal your husband's level of sincerity to you. Because, hard as it will be, if he is genuinely remorseful and seeks forgiveness for a slip or a relapse, God tells you to forgive no matter how many times your husband stumbles.

But how do you know when enough is enough? I'm treading very carefully here because my prayer is that your marriage can experience full restoration, but there are times when that is not possible. There is no neat formula to apply to your experience to determine whether you should stay in your marriage or not. However, God's Word does give us direction.

Before you even contemplate a separation or divorce, it's important for you to go through the three different levels of confrontation that Jesus laid out in Matthew 18.

Read Matthew 18:15–17.	Level of Confrontation
"If your brother sins against you, go and tell him his fault, between you and him alone. If he listens to you, you have gained your brother."	When your heart is in the right place and you are able to confront with love and grace, go to your husband alone and define the issue. Let him know his behavior is sinful and it is hurting you and your family. Moreover, it violates God's design for marriage. Assure him you are eager to forgive and work toward the restoration of your marriage as soon as he confesses and repents before the Lord, asks for

forgiveness from you, and demonstrates sincere, obvious intentions to seek help. Have phone numbers with you for counselors, treatment centers, and support groups.

"But if he does not listen, take one or two others along with you, that every charge may be established by the evidence of two or three witnesses."

If your husband refuses to own or address his pornography addiction, you need to share what's going on with two or three others. They need to go with you to confront your husband again. Use wisdom and discernment in choosing these people. They should be mature Christians who are willing to support both of you. Often, the shame of having someone outside your immediate family know about his struggle with pornography is enough to stop your husband's downward spiral. Again, be ready with support numbers and be prepared to begin individual and marriage counseling right away.

"If he refuses to listen to them, tell it to the church. And if he refuses to listen even to the church, let him be to you as a Gentile and a tax collector."

If neither of the first two levels of confrontation has succeeded in turning your husband's heart, you need to involve your church. Again, use discernment here. I encourage you to begin with a pastor, particularly the pastor who typically oversees counseling and care. This pastor will take another leader or representative from the church to confront your husband about his sin and (God willing) offer help. (See appendix B.)

243

I know this sounds very matter-of-fact and terrifying at the same time. I'm sorry. There is absolutely nothing easy about this.

If your husband is still not willing to make changes after the third level of confrontation, one option for you to consider is a separation. Separating from your husband may create the crisis necessary for him to seek help and finally work toward restoration. The goal of your separation is still the restoration of your marriage. Sometimes it is better to love an unrepentant person from a distance. You *are* loving your husband by taking difficult action in the hope that it will compel him to draw close to the One who can pluck him out of the slimy pit.

Think of it this way: the greatest gift you can give your husband is to love God more than you love your husband. God can redeem your husband; you cannot. Thus you love him more by loving in light of his need to repent.

There may be circumstances that make it necessary to move directly from the third level of confrontation to the consideration of divorce. I want you to know what God says about this.

Read Matthew 19:9. Circle Jesus' words that make divorce an acceptable option.

> "And I say to you: whoever divorces his wife, except for sexual immorality, and marries another, commits adultery."

The Greek word used for "sexual immorality" is *porneia* (por-nā'-ä), the root of our contemporary word "pornography." The Easton Bible Dictionary says, ". . . much of the behavior that is fairly acceptable in our culture is exactly what Paul would term 'porneia.' Sexual immorality. Like what? Like premarital sex. Like sex outside of marriage. Like pornography. Like prostitution."[2] This Greek word is used in the New Testament thirty-two times, which points to the importance of addressing this sin issue. Don't misunderstand. God is not saying that you *must* divorce, but it is an option.

Before you make the decision to divorce, it is especially important to examine the hearts of everyone involved. Ask God to make you completely transparent in this exercise.

Examine *your* heart. On a scale of 1–10, how forgiving have you been toward your husband?

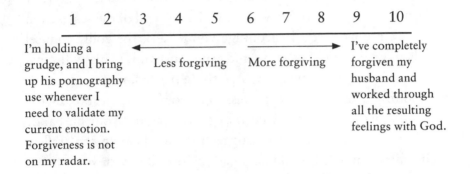

| 1 | 2 | 3 | 4 | 5 | 6 | 7 | 8 | 9 | 10 |

I'm holding a grudge, and I bring up his pornography use whenever I need to validate my current emotion. Forgiveness is not on my radar.

Less forgiving ← → More forgiving

I've completely forgiven my husband and worked through all the resulting feelings with God.

Examine *his* heart (as evidenced by his behavior). On a scale of 1–10, how repentant has your husband been?

| 1 | 2 | 3 | 4 | 5 | 6 | 7 | 8 | 9 | 10 |

Despite going through all three levels of confrontation, he is unaccepting of responsibility, unremorseful, unrepentant, and unwilling to stop his addiction.

Relapses happen often and for greater lengths of time. I wonder if he even wants to change.

Slips are less and less frequent, and we always talk about them. I can tell he is really trying to overcome his addiction.

He has completely taken ownership of his sin, has confessed and repented before God, and has sought my forgiveness.

I pray that you are both working your way toward the right end of that scale, toward a ten. If so, you are on your way toward restoration and healing with the help of Jehovah Rophe—"The LORD, your healer" (Exodus 15:22–26).

If, however, you find *your* numbers to be on the lower end of the scale (regardless of where your husband's numbers fall), *you* need some help. Please seek counseling immediately. Intentionally or unintentionally, you may be sabotaging any hope your marriage has of restoration. If this is you, then, frankly, you are in the pit of sin yourself.

Divorce enters the picture if your heart is operating near the high end of the scale, with continuous movement toward ten, while your husband's heart is operating very near the low end of the scale. Even in these circumstances, I encourage you to seek the godly counsel of others who know both you and your husband. (This will most likely *not* be a family member.) Ask these trusted, mature counselors (faithful friend, pastor, professional counselor) to look at the scale you just marked. How do *they* score you and your husband? Do they have any insights or suggestions for healing that reflect their unique knowledge and personal relationship with you?

In the end, the decision is solely yours, though the decision will affect those you love most. Pray as you have never prayed before. As you sense God's leading, move forward in the direction he encourages you to go. Know this: God has an intended design for marriage.

> Therefore a man shall leave his father and his mother
> and hold fast to his wife, and they shall become one flesh.
> (Genesis 2:24)

It is a design for oneness, grace, and mercy that is a model of our relationship with Christ (Ephesians 5:31–33). As long as your husband is unrepentant and continuing in his sin, despite every effort you have made to extend grace and mercy as his helpmate, you will never know the fullness of God's intended design in your marriage.

Take some time to pull back from the chaos of your life and settle into a cozy spot with your Bible, your journal, and Jesus. Ask him how he sees the condition of your heart and your husband's heart. If all is well, give him abundant praise for the work he has done in your marriage. If he reveals that things are not well with your heart, ask him to place his healing hand on your wounded, disgruntled heart and make it whole. If you are standing ready to forgive but your husband chooses to persist in his sin, ask the Father to lead you on the path you should go. He knows the way that is best for you. God said, "I have loved you with an everlasting love" (Jeremiah 31:3).

Day 4: Creating an Environment of Healing

I asked the question, "What have you and your husband done to create an environment of healing?"

Gotten on our knees together frequently.

—Rebecca

We have often prayed about the addiction, trust issues, and the impact on our family. He has a series of accountability partners, and he's learned a number of other strategies that will help him not fall into temptation. Though I do become hurt and upset when he slips, I try to come back with an attitude of forgiveness and prayer so that we can continue to move forward in healing, not backward.

—Natalie

The biggest thing we both have learned from our mistakes is that neither of us is going to bail on our relationship. There was so much fear before that we couldn't be honest with each other about anything. We feel the weight of each other's commitment and it helps us share without fear. "Perfect love casts out fear." Our love isn't perfect, but it's sure a lot closer than it was.

—Lynne

(After years of her husband's pornography addiction, Lynne almost left her husband. Instead, she removed her heart from the relationship and a couple of years later ended up having an affair herself. Lynne and her husband are healing from both betrayals.)

Well, we have not received Victoria's Secret catalogs at our house for quite some time!

—Lisa

I moved to a new condo. I set very clear boundaries, that I am not willing to even speak to my husband unless he is willing to be totally honest. Each time I opened the door to talk, it was just more lies.

—Sarah

(Sarah's husband of one year has taken no ownership of his addiction. He has gone so far as to bring prostitutes home. This week he asked to end the marriage.)

While forgiveness is essential for healing a heart trampled by sexual betrayal, there are additional ways a wife can promote healing in her marriage and her heart, assuming her husband is repentant and equally eager for restoration. Insanity is doing the same things over and over but expecting different results. This is why we don't forget when we forgive. You look back at where God has taken you and learn new steps for your future. You can't become the wife God desires without the lessons you've learned in the past serving as a strong, solid core for your mosaic heart of the future. That's the beauty of God's economy: nothing he has allowed in your past is excessive or unnecessary because he uses it all for his glory.

While the intent of this book is to walk with you on *your* journey of spiritual healing, not to serve as a playbook for how to restore your marriage, I would be remiss if I didn't share some specific things you can do to create an environment of healing in your marriage. Your spiritual healing may result in positive benefits to your marriage, but the reverse is also true. Creating an environment of healing for your marriage can increase the opportunities for your heart to mend as well.

The most important thing you can do is fix your eyes on God and trust him for the work he is doing in your marriage and in your heart. You have already been doing this as you worked through this book. If you think about it, I didn't often tell you to pray and see what God has to say. I took you by the hand to God's Word, creating opportunities for you to commune with him.

One bonus that comes with focusing on God is that when you're considering what he is capable of doing in your situation, your mind is not free to obsess over your husband's daily choices. That is not to say you aren't noticing your man's efforts. When you are tempted to scrutinize your husband's actions, concentrate on the positive—believe the best about him. Consider the person God created him to be and nurture your love for *that* man. Your husband is a work in progress, just as you are. Don't let his underdeveloped characteristics distort your opinion of who he is in Christ. Stop holding him hostage under your condemning eyes, which continue to label him "unfaithful." Even though the label fit at one time, see him as God's work in progress and he will have more freedom to become a husband according to God's design. (In other words, back off. Let him get up.)

Describe the man you believe God is creating in your husband. Remember to believe the best about him.

Find ways to talk with your husband about true intimacy. Talking about it is the first step toward experiencing it.

Don't tiptoe around the topic of your husband's struggle with pornography. I'm not suggesting that you talk about it daily, but do talk about it. Even when your husband has been "sober" from his porn addiction for weeks, months, or years, it's good to ask now and then, "How are you doing with _____?" You might fill in that blank with "pornography . . . lust . . . masturbation . . . your struggle with the Internet," or you and your husband might settle on a "term" for the addiction. I know of a couple who referred to the husband's struggle as "Lou." Having a neutral name for the addiction removed the negative emotion and pain still associated with that hateful, old scoundrel. (They never were fond of Lou.)

What would you like this transparency about the addiction to look like in your marriage? Does it already look like this or is this a goal?

True intimacy includes creating safe opportunities to discuss every struggle together—yours as well as his. Share the condition of your heart with each other when there is joy, fear, confusion, anger, and temptation. Take those concerns and battles to the foot of the cross as a couple. Ask God to stand with you as you wrestle with difficult things. Together, you can grow in this uncomfortable place.

If you expect different behavior from your husband, you may need to set boundaries against pornography in your home and marriage. Be careful! These boundaries can begin to look like you are exacting revenge if they are not handled with grace and a forgiving spirit.

Describe boundaries that you (and your husband) have set to keep your marriage pure. Can you support those boundaries with Scripture?

Boundary   Supporting Scripture

Remember, setting boundaries is not an act of vengeance. It is a way to work together to build a wall that will protect the sanctity of your marriage. Let me suggest a few boundaries.[1]

- Allow no coarse jokes or hints of immorality. Be extremely sensitive to sexually charged media or resources in your home. Ask yourself, "How will watching this program or movie, or having this magazine or advertisement in our home affect our walk with God?"

  But sexual immorality and all impurity or covetousness must not even be named among you, as is proper among saints. Let there be no filthiness nor foolish talk nor crude joking, which are out of place, but instead let there be thanksgiving. (Ephesians 5:3–4)

- Keep the marriage bed pure.

  Let marriage be held in honor among all, and let the marriage bed be undefiled, for God will judge the sexually immoral and adulterous. (Hebrews 13:4)

- Do not initiate sexual intimacy if there is unresolved conflict.

  For this is the will of God, your sanctification: that you abstain from sexual immorality; that each one of you know how to control his own body in holiness and honor, not in the passion of lust like the Gentiles who do not know God . . . . (1 Thessalonians 4:3–5)

- Don't be tally keepers, keeping a record of wrongs.

  > If you, LORD, kept a record of sins,
  > Lord, who could stand?
  > But with you there is forgiveness,
  > so that we can, with reverence, serve you.
  > (Psalm 130:3–4 NIV)

- Remember, God has given Someone else the task of conviction of sin. You are not responsible for your husband's daily choices. Your job is to walk in obedience to the Word.

  > Nevertheless, I tell you the truth: it is to your
  >   advantage that I go away,
  > for if I do not go away, the Helper will not come
  >   to you.
  > But if I go, I will send him to you. And when
  >   he comes,
  > he will convict the world concerning sin and
  >   righteousness and judgment:

concerning sin, because they do not believe in me;
concerning righteousness, because I go to the Father,
and you will see me no longer; concerning judgment,
because the ruler of this world is judged.
(John 16:7–11)

Journal Assignment:

Ask God to supply you with the grace to adopt the motto "Out
with the old, in with the new" in order to create a healing
environment for your marriage.

Name the *old* patterns of behavior that you need to toss out.

Claim the *new* patterns you need to graft in.

Therefore, if anyone is in Christ, he is a new creation.
The old has passed away; behold, the new has come.
(2 Corinthians 5:17)

Praise be to God!

Day 5: He Sees and He Redeems

Dear Daughter,

I know you desire your marriage to be healed, and you never saw this coming. You trusted me. Your trust has not been misplaced. I have told you for a while that "I am doing a new thing." I am—in you and in your husband.

The time will come when you will see the unveiling of this new thing. You have seen glimpses of it, like a master artist working on a fine mosaic. You have stolen a peek and seen me picking out the beautiful broken fragments of your heart and carefully arranging them into my new design for your heart. Smoothing rough edges, gently shaping fragile pieces, fitting them together in an unfamiliar but pleasing pattern, cementing, and polishing . . . but I am not done. You must wait and let the Artist complete the job. Masterpieces take time.

All you see now is the mess. I, however, am focused on the work before me. I don't even notice the disarray and debris. The creative process is before me, and I have all my energy invested in it. I am passionate for your new mosaic heart to be exquisite, sturdy, and whole.

Love,
Your Heavenly Father

I am proud of you for the work you have done in the pages of this book, but how *I* feel isn't what's at stake here. God sees your efforts too, and I can't wait to see what he's going to do next.

> What no eye has seen, nor ear heard,
> nor the heart of man imagined,
> what God has prepared for those who love him. . . .
> (1 Corinthians 2:9)

Do you remember the story of Abram, Sarai, and Hagar? God promises Abram an heir, but years pass, and when Abram is eighty-five years old, he has yet to hold an heir in his arms. Abram's wife Sarai takes matters into her own hands and offers her maidservant Hagar to Abram. Sarai misinterprets God's delay as his denial, and she comes down with a serious case of "The Hagar Syndrome."

Have you ever had a case of "The Hagar Syndrome" during this journey of your broken heart? Have you misinterpreted God's seeming delay in changing your husband as a denial of assistance, so you thought it wise to give him some help in the matter? Make note of it here.

Would you rather remember this season of suffering and renewal as one marked by all the great things *you* have done or all the great things *God* has done? Why?

Hagar conceives and (surprise, surprise!) Sarai is jealous. "Then Sarai dealt harshly with [Hagar], and she fled from her" (Genesis 16:6b). The tendency to run shouldn't come as a surprise, given that "Hagar" means *flight*. As Hagar is running away, who do you suppose she runs into? None other than the Lord. He finds her near a spring "on the way to Shur" (Genesis 16:7).

This is exactly why I love to study God's Word, because he leaves nothing to chance. No wasted words. None. The word "Shur" means *wall*. How appropriate! Hagar is pregnant as a result of *Sarai's* need to get ahead of God. She's in the wilderness, and she most likely feels like her back is up against a wall. Been there?

Have you attempted to run away (physically, emotionally, mentally) from the difficult circumstances you are in, only to have God meet you when you feel most alone in the wilderness? What was that like?

The Lord graciously encourages Hagar in her distress and sends her back home with a promise to redeem her and her descendants. God names her unborn son Ishmael, meaning "God who hears." In turn, Hagar does something that no one else in Scripture does. She names God *El Roi*—the God Who Sees.

> So she called the name of the Lord who spoke to her,
> "You are a God of seeing," for she said,
> "Truly here I have seen him who looks after me."
> (Genesis 16:13)

Can you comprehend the despair Hagar experiences years later when she and her son, now a teenager, are cast out of Abraham and Sarah's home and sent to wander in the wilderness of Beersheba (Genesis 21:14)? When the skin of water is wrung dry, Hagar puts her son under a bush and, heartbroken, moves out of sight so as not to watch him die.

She did not ask for this! Is she disposable? Surely she must be worthless. The father of her child doesn't want her anymore. Her heart is shattered, and the fragments are scattered across the barren wilderness.

I don't need to ask if you can imagine how she felt. I know. You know. But lean in, because we are about to be reminded of the truth Hagar learned in the wilderness, and you won't want to miss this. *God's faithfulness is greater than man's unfaithfulness.*

And the angel of God called to Hagar from heaven and said to her, "What troubles you, Hagar? Fear not, for God has heard the voice of the boy where he is. Up! Lift up the boy, and hold him fast with your hand, for I will make him into a great nation." (Genesis 21:17–18)

The God who _____ is also the God who _____.

How have you experienced the God who sees and hears?

If you were to give a name to God, what would it be and why?

Day 5: He Sees and He Redeems

Read Matthew 6:4, 6, 18:

> . . . so that your giving may be in secret. And your Father who sees in secret will reward you.

> But when you pray, go into your room and shut the door and pray to your Father who is in secret. And your Father who sees in secret will reward you.

> . . . that your fasting may not be seen by others but by your Father who is in secret. And your Father who sees in secret will reward you.

These verses assure you that your Father still _____

> This is the confidence that we have toward him,
> that if we ask anything according to his will he hears us.
> (1 John 5:14)

. . . and he still _____.

The truth that your God sees and hears, and that his faithfulness is greater than your husband's unfaithfulness, is a truth you must not keep to yourself. Your broken heart has been on a long journey of healing. Don't keep it to yourself.

> Blessed be the God and Father of our Lord Jesus Christ,
> the Father of mercies and the God of all comfort,
> who comforts us in all our affliction,
> so that we may be able to comfort those who are in any affliction,
> with the comfort with which we ourselves are comforted by God.
> For as we share abundantly in Christ's sufferings,
> so through Christ we share abundantly in comfort too.
> (2 Corinthians 1:3–5)

Just as Hagar's story of a broken heart can be used today for your good, God will use your story of a broken heart for someone else's good. Believe me, in the midst of *my* crisis, I would never have believed it. I do now.

In the first chapter of this book, I told you "God had to expose what was going on with your husband for you to rebuild on a firm foundation."

[He] will bring to light the things now hidden in darkness
and will disclose the purposes of the heart. (1 Corinthians 4:5)

While the revealing of your husband's sexual addiction pulled the rug out from under you, it came as no surprise to the Almighty. He sees the sins committed in a darkened office or bedroom just as clearly as those done in broad daylight. We know this to be true because our God sees.

Now we find ourselves at the end of our journey together. My work is done. Yours may or may not be. Trust his timing. Journey back through the pages of this book and linger in the pages of your journal.

During the darkest days of your journey, the Artist is at work.

But whoever does what is true comes to the light,
so that it may be clearly seen that his works have been carried
out in God.
(John 3:21)

Arise, shine, for your light has come,
and the glory of the LORD has risen upon you.
(Isaiah 60:1)

One day soon as you stand in the Light, you will see that in the dark chaos of this season he has picked up the pieces of your shattered heart and joined them together with hope, faith, encouragement, and his presence. He has created in you a new mosaic heart that reflects the extravagant beauty of himself.

Appendix A

Resources

(I recommend beginning with the starred ones.)

Books

Carnes, Stefanie, ed. *Mending a Shattered Heart: A Guide for Partners of Sex Addicts*. Carefree, AZ: Gentle Path Press, 2008.

Cloud, Henry and John Townsend. *Boundaries: When to Say Yes, When to Say No to Take Control of Your Life*. Grand Rapids: Zondervan, 1992.

Dobson, James C. *Love Must Be Tough: New Hope for Families in Crisis*. Nashville: Thomas Nelson Publishing, 1996.

Gallagher, Kathy. *When His Secret Sin Breaks Your Heart: Letters to Hurting Wives*. Dry Ridge, KY: Pure Life Ministries, 2003.

*Laaser, Debra. *Shattered Vows: Hope and Healing for Women Who Have Been Sexually Betrayed*. Grand Rapids: Zondervan, 2008.

Christian Websites

www.bebroken.com. This website offers education, support, hope, and healing to the sexually broken and their wives.

www.freedombeginshere.org. This ministry creates and provides resources to help in the battle for purity and restoration when it comes to pornography and sexual sin.

www.harvestusa.org. Harvest USA brings the truth and mercy of Jesus Christ to help men, women, and families affected by sexual struggles and sin and equips churches to reach out to sexually broken people.

www.marriagebuilders.com. Dr. Willard F. Harley Jr. offers information to help married couples deal with unresolved conflict, with specific information on infidelity.

www.pornaddicthubby.com. This website offers resources for wives and girlfriends of Internet pornography addicts.

*www.pureintimacy.org. Focus on the Family's website (Dr. James Dobson) has a great deal of information about intimacy, sexual addiction, and sexuality in general.

www.puritycoalition.org. This website of the National Coalition for Purity is a nondenominational organization that links Christian individuals, churches, and businesses to stand strong for sexual purity. Irv Woolf is the director, and his wife, Elsie, directs the Women of Truth ministry.

www.settingcaptivesfree.com. Pure Life Ministry's website offers free courses and resources to help gain freedom from sexual addiction, as well as courses for wives of addicts.

www.sexhelp.com. Patrick Carnes's website offers online tests for spouses of sexual addicts and other resources.

Support Groups and Workshops

www.bethesdaworkshops.org. Offers healing workshops for sexual addicts and their spouses.

www.cosa-recovery.org. COSA is a twelve-step recovery program for women and men whose lives have been affected by another person's compulsive sexual behavior. Find a meeting near you.

www.faithfulandtruemarriages.org. Offers three-day intensives for spouses of sex addicts.

www.faithfulandtrueministries.com. Dr. Mark Laaser and Debra Laaser provide counseling, education, and support for sexual addicts and their spouses.

www.freedomeveryday.org. L.I.F.E. Ministries (Living in Freedom Everyday) provides a list of support groups in the United States who use their L.I.F.E. guides.

www.loveandrespect.com. Dr. Emerson Eggerichs and his team offer marriage intensives to help couples overcome seemingly insurmountable marital problems.

www.marriage-encounter.org. This national ministry offers two- or three-day weekend encounters, giving spouses an opportunity to grow in their marriage through open and honest communication.

www.newlifepartners.org. Christian online resource and peer support group for women whose lives have been impacted by husbands or loved ones caught in the web of pornography and/or sexual addiction. This is not a counseling group.

*www.purelifealliance.org. This website helps people find healing communities—support groups, counselors, and resources.

www.purelifeministries.org. Pure Life Ministries website, live-in and at-home programs, weekend events, help for wives, articles, links, and resources (Christian perspective).

www.sexaddict.com. Heart to Heart Ministries website, telephone and on-site counseling, spousal help, links, and resources (Christian perspective).

Professional Counseling

www.christiananswers.net/love/supportgroups.html. Christian website that lists several of the most notable organizations providing professional counseling.

www.safefamilies.org. Professional counseling resources for recovery and pornography addiction.

Internet Filters

There are three types of Internet filtering software: voluntary, visible, and stealth.

Voluntary software is for those who decide to share their struggle with an accountability partner. (This should *not* be the spouse!) This is not a filter, but it is free.

www.X3watch.com

Visible filtering software can be seen on the computer, and it may be tempting to disable it.

www.covenanteyes.com

*www.internetfilterreview.com. This is a great place to compare Internet filtering software.

www.netnanny.com

www.safeeyes.com. Accountability and filter.

Stealth filtering software is not easily seen on the computer. It is accurate and difficult to disable.

www.webwatchernow.com

www.spectorsoft.com

www.keyghost.com

Appendix B

When Your Church Is Not behind You

I am well aware that some churches take the "medicate the symptoms" rather than the "acknowledge and address the disease" approach when faced with issues like pornography and advanced levels of sexual addiction in the family. Unfortunately, the "peace at any price" syndrome has taken deep root in the evangelical church. Let's review what Scripture says the church's response should look like.

It is actually reported that there is sexual immorality
    among you,
and of a kind that is not tolerated even among pagans,
for a man has his father's wife.
And you are arrogant!
Ought you not rather to mourn?
Let him who has done this be removed from among you.
For though absent in body, I am present in spirit;
and as if present, I have already pronounced judgment
on the one who did such a thing.
When you are assembled in the name of the Lord Jesus and my
    spirit is present,
with the power of our Lord Jesus,
you are to deliver this man to Satan for the destruction of
    the flesh,
so that his spirit may be saved in the day of the Lord.
(1 Corinthians 5:1–5)

In this passage, Paul has heard that a member of the Corinthian church is engaging in sexual sin. Paul condemns the church for being "proud" or "arrogant" about the situation. (I can't help wondering if the man was part of church leadership or prominent in the community. We don't know, but it might explain why they opted for tolerance instead of discipline. Perhaps they simply didn't want to get their hands dirty.)

Paul firmly tells the church to "deliver this man to Satan for the destruction of the flesh, *so that* his spirit may be saved in the day of the Lord" (v.5, italics mine). Notice that Paul doesn't dance around the sin and tell the man he needs therapy (though I would argue that many in this situation need counseling—and fast!). The church's purpose for disciplining the sinner harshly is for his restoration in the Lord.

What's more, following Paul's instruction worked.

Now if anyone has caused pain, he has caused it not to me,
but in some measure—not to put it too severely—to all of you.
For such a one, this punishment by the majority is enough,
so you should rather turn to forgive and comfort him,
or he may be overwhelmed by excessive sorrow.
So I beg you to reaffirm your love for him.
(2 Corinthians 2:5–8)

If you are following the model of confrontation set out in Matthew 18 and your church is not behind you, you must ask what their motivation is for tolerating sexual sin. Saving a relationship between the man and the church is not enough reason to disobey God's Word. Perhaps it is time to seek a new church home.

Notes

Week 1 Day 1: Truth Unveiled

1. Martin Bashir and Steven Baker, "Sex Addict Leads Secret Life Online," *ABC News/Nightline,* posted May 19, 2009, accessed November 27, 2010, http://www.abcnews.go.com/Nightline/story?id =7624099&page=1.

Week 1 Day 4: When the Wind Blows

1. Margaret Clarkson, *Destined for Glory* (Grand Rapids: Wm. B. Eerdmans, 1983), 87.
2. Ibid.

Week 1 Day 5: Today We Fight!

1. "Happily Never After: New PTC Study Reveals TV Favors Non-Marital Sex," Parents Television Council, posted August 5, 2008, accessed November 27, 2010, http://www.parentstv.org/ptc/news/ release/2008/0805.asp.

Week 2 Day 1: Let Go of Being a Pleaser

1. Spiros Zodhiates, *The Complete Word Study Dictionary New Testament* (Chattanooga: AMG, 1992), 120.

Week 2 Day 4: Let Go of Guilt

1. *Merriam-Webster Dictionary Online,* s.v. "Guilt," accessed October 8, 2010, http://www.merriam-webster.com/dictionary/guilt.
2. Dietrich Bonhoeffer, *The Cost of Discipleship* (New York: Macmillan, 1959), 44–45.

Week 2 Day 5: Let Go of Anger

1. David A. Seamands, *Healing for Damaged Emotions* (Colorado Springs: David C. Cook, 1981), 96.

Week 3 Day 1: Lies, Lies, and More Lies

1. *Wikipedia,* s.v. "Betrayal," last modified March 19, 2012.
2. Janis Abrahams, *After the Affair* (New York: HarperCollins, 1997), 149–150. I have written an amended version of Abraham's "Trust-Enhancing Behaviors."

Week 3 Day 2: Well-Placed Trust

1. Helen Keller, *The Story of My Life* (Middlesex, Great Britain: The Echo Library, 2007), 141.

Week 3 Day 3: Safe Support

1. "Evangelicals Are Addicted to Porn," ChristiaNet, accessed October 15, 2010, http://www.Christiannews.christianet.com/1154951956.htm.

Week 3 Day 5: Needs, Desires, Longings, and Yearnings

1. John and Stasi Eldredge, *Captivating: Unveiling the Mystery of a Woman's Soul* (Nashville: Thomas Nelson, 2005), 42.
2. *Encarta World English Dictionary* [World English Edition], s.v. "Nurture," accessed March 19, 2012, http://www.bing.com/Dictionary/search?q=nurture&qs=ds&form=QB.
3. *9quotes* entry for "Michelangelo," accessed November 5, 2010, http://9quotes.com/Michelangelo.
4. Dacher Keltner, "Hands On Research: The Science of Touch," *Greater Good,* posted September 29, 2010, accessed November 27, 2010, http://www.greatergood.berkeley.edu/article/item/hands_on_research/.

Week 4 Day 1: Pursued and Chosen

1. *Encarta World English Dictionary,* s.v. "Identity," accessed March 19, 2012, http://www.bing.com/Dictionary/search?q=identity&qs=ds&form=QB.
2. Mark R. Laaser, *Healing the Wounds of Sexual Addiction* (Grand Rapids: Zondervan, 1999), 88.

Notes

Week 4 Day 3: Comparison Trap

1. "Cosmetic Plastic Surgery Spending Increases 9 Percent to $12.4 Billion," *Aesthetic Medicine News,* posted in 2009, accessed November 22, 2011, http://www.aestheticmedicinenews.com/cosmetic-plastic-surgery-spending-increases-9-percent-to-124-billion.htm.

Week 4 Day 5: Irreplaceable

1. *Encarta World English Dictionary,* s.v. "Union," accessed March 19, 2010, http://www.bing.com/Dictionary/search?q=union&qs=ds&form=QB.
2. *Encarta World English Dictionary,* s.v. "Lust," accessed March 19, 2010, http://www.bing.com/Dictionary/search?q=lust&qs=ds&form=QB.
3. Brennan Manning, *The Furious Longing of God* (Colorado Springs: David C. Cook, 2009), 65.
4. Paulo Coelho, *The Alchemist: A Graphic Novel* (New York: HarperOne, 2010), 128.
5. Jamison J. Statema, "You're My Little Girl" (Fun Attic Music, 2001).

Week 5 Day 1: Black-and-White Thinking

1. Blue Letter Bible, "The Major Prophet Isaiah 57—(ESV—English Standard Version)." Blue Letter Bible. 1996–2012, accessed March 19, 2012, http://www.blueletterbible.org/Bible.cfm?b=Isa&c=57&v=15&t=ESV#conc/15.
2. *International Standard Bible Encyclopedia* (Grand Rapids: Wm. B. Eerdmans, 1915), s.v. "Contrite."

Week 5 Day 3: Pick It Up to Lay It Down

1. Antonio Porchia, *Voices* (Chicago: First Copper Canyon, 1969), 7.
2. Gary Thomas, *Sacred Marriage* (Grand Rapids: Zondervan, 2000), 96.
3. Jennifer Kennedy Dean, *He Restores My Soul: A Forty-Day Journey Toward Personal Renewal* (Nashville: Broadman & Holman, 1999), 27.

Week 5 Day 4: Go Through It or Grow Through It

1. Henri J. M. Nouwen, *The Way of the Heart* (New York: HarperCollins, 1981), 20.

2. Margaret Clarkson, *Grace Grows Best in Winter* (Grand Rapids: Zondervan, 1984), 85.

3. Sarah Young, *Jesus Calling* (Nashville: Thomas Nelson, 2004), 369.

4. Robert Collen, "Look! It is winter," *Burning World: Poems* (Athol, MA: Haleys, 1997), 47.

Week 5 Day 5: A New Mosaic

1. *Encarta World English Dictionary,* s.v. "Mosaic," accessed March 19, 2012, http://www.bing.com/Dictionary/search?q=mosaic&qs=ds&form=QB.

2. *Encarta World English Dictionary,* s.v. "Pressure Cooker," accessed March 19, 2012, http://www.bing.com/Dictionary/search?q=define+pressure+cooker&qpvt=pressure+cooker+definition&FORM=DTPDIA.

Week 6 Day 1: A Choice

1. Dietrich Bonhoeffer, *The Cost of Discipleship* (New York: Macmillan, 1959), 44–45

2. Ardel B. Caneday, "A Biblical Primer and Grammar on Forgiveness of Sin," accessed March 19, 2012, http://www.scribd.com/full/19840923?access_key=key-gp3oz3pczepq0zf4aux.

3. Neil T. Anderson, *The Steps to Freedom in Christ* (Ventura, CA: Gospel Light, 1990), 11.

4. Dallas Willard, *The Divine Conspiracy: Rediscovering Our Old Hidden Life in God* (New York: HarperOne, 1998), 221.

Week 6 Day 3: The Hard Truth

1. Debra Laaser, *Shattered Vows* (Grand Rapids: Zondervan, 2008), 194.

2. *Easton's Bible Dictionary,* s.v. "Fornication," accessed November 27, 2010, http://www.studylight.org/dic/ebd/view.cgi?word=fornication&action=Lookup.

Week 6 Day 4: Creating an Environment of Healing

1. Robin Weidner, "Did God Really Say? Setting Godly Boundaries in Marriage," *Focus on the Family,* posted 2008, accessed November 27, 2010, http://www.focusonthefamily.com/marriage/sex_and_intimacy/building_a_pure_marriage/did_god_really_say.aspx.

TRUTH & MERCY

Harvest USA brings the truth and mercy of Jesus Christ to men, women, and families affected by sexual sin and equips the church to minister to sexually broken people. We are a faith-operated, missions ministry. Most of our work is given freely or at low cost. We are primarily supported by churches and individuals convinced of our mission.

If you have found this book helpful, consider partnering with us by giving financially, advocating for our ministry in your church, and/or by volunteering your time. For questions, counsel, and opportunities to help, please contact:

3901B Main Street, Suite 304
Philadelphia, PA 19127
215.482.0111
info@harvestusa.org
www.harvestusa.org

For Harvest USA resources visit **www.harvest-usa-store.com**
or call 336.378.7775